Contents

My name is Shaka Zulu

It is 1828, and very soon I will die. My people have had enough of me, even my brothers; they are coming now armed with spears. I am a very powerful man, and powerful men have enemies, I know that. It is true that I have killed many people and ordered the deaths of many more, some who did not deserve it. But blood had to spill to make the Zulu nation great and to show people I am strong.

I have been thinking back with pride at my achievements. Can you imagine that I was born unwanted by my father and our people? That I learned how to fight and lead warriors in a vast Zulu army? Now my name is known throughout Africa and across seas. I am Shaka Zulu.

I am king of my people and a hero. People will remember me in the future.

HERO JOURNALS

Shaka Zulu

Richard Spilsbury

Raintree is an imprint of Capstone Global Library Limited, a company incorporated in England and Wales having its registered office at 7 Pilgrim Street, London, EC4V 6LB – Registered company number: 6695582

www.raintreepublishers.co.uk
myorders@raintreepublishers.co.uk

Edited by Adam Miller, Charlotte Guillain, and Claire Throp
Designed by Richard Parker and Ken Vail Graphic Design
Original illustrations © Capstone Global Library Ltd 2014
Illustrated by Stathis Petropoulos
Picture research Tracy Cummins
Production by Victoria Fitzgerald
Originated by Capstone Global Library Ltd
Printed and bound in China by CTPS

ISBN 978 1 406 26572 9 (hardback)
17 16 15 14 13
10 9 8 7 6 5 4 3 2 1

ISBN 978 1 406 26579 8 (paperback)
18 17 16 15 14
10 9 8 7 6 5 4 3 2 1

British Library Cataloguing in Publication Data
Spilsbury, Richard
Shaka Zulu. – (Hero journals)
968.4'039'092-dc23
A full catalogue record for this book is available from the British Library.

Acknowledgements
We would like to thank the following for permission to reproduce photographs: Alamy pp. 23 (© FVE Media), 28 (© 19th era), 32 (© Mary Evans Picture Library/Alamy); Bridgeman Art Library pp. 4, 14, 22, 37, 38 (© Look and Learn), 6 (© The Stapleton Collection), 33 (© Ken Welsh), 35 (The Diary of Henry Francis Fynn after original sketch by Henry Francis Fynn); Corbis pp. 5 (© Mike Hutchings/Reuters), 9 (© Martin Harvey), 13 (© Selwyn Tait/Sygma); Getty Images pp. 11 (Ami Vitale), 16 (Daryl Balfour), 24-25 (Keystone Features), 26 (Volkmar K. Wentzel/National Geographic), 31 (Roger de la Harpe), 39 (Heinrich van den Berg); Shutterstock pp. 27 bottom (© Joe Mercier), 27 top (© Tim UR); Superstock pp. 17 (Bill Gozansky/age fotostock), 20 (Universal Images Group).

Design elements supplied by Shutterstock (© R-studio), (© Pavel K), (© Picsfive), (© karawan).

Cover photograph of Shaka Zulu restaurant statue in Camden, reproduced with permission of Alamy (© Tim Gainey).

Every effort has been made to contact copyright holders of material reproduced in this book. Any omissions will be rectified in subsequent printings if notice is given to the publisher.

The leader of the Zulu people in South Africa today is King Goodwill Zwelithini. Today's Zulus are part of an integrated South Africa. Zwelithini leads by promoting his people and their customs.

> *"Up! Children of Zulu, your day has come. Up! And destroy them all."*
>
> Shaka Zulu

Legacy

Shaka Zulu was a tyrant, but one of the greatest military leaders Africa has ever known. Through his leadership, Zulu power expanded from a clan living in an area of around 259 square kilometres (100 square miles) to a vast nation covering over 29,784 square kilometres (11,000 square miles). Today, there are around 10 million descendants of these Zulus in South Africa.

The early years

I was born in 1787 in south-eastern Africa. I am the son of Senzangakona, king of the Zulu people. My mother's name is Nandi. She is the daughter of a chief of the Langeni people who live near by.

We live in a place called EmaKhosini, or Burial-place of the Kings. You see, my Zulu ancestors have lived here for centuries. My people say that our first king was called Zulu. This means heaven. He came from further north, where it was hot and dry. He settled at EmaKhosini because it was a green place with rivers. It is a good place to keep cattle and grow crops.

Our families lived in simple huts made from grasses.

Our neighbours

The area ruled by my father Senzangakona — the Zulu chiefdom — is one of hundreds in these parts. Every chiefdom has a different chief and contains different clans. Our nearest neighbours are the Langeni people, and their chiefdom is bigger than ours. The older Zulus are always telling me and the other children not to stray too often onto the land of neighbouring chiefdoms. We know this could lead to trouble and even deadly fighting.

People of southern Africa

Thousands of years ago, the southern African people were mostly small groups of hunter-gatherers. During the following centuries, different tribes who were cattle herders and farmers moved south from central Africa in search of land. One tribe called the Nguni settled in South Africa from around 300 BC. The Zulu and Langeni chiefdoms were part of this tribe.

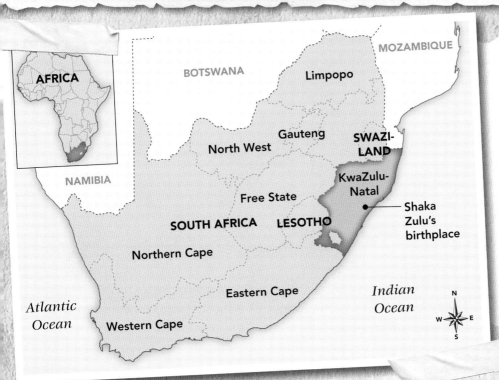

Shaka was born not far from the coast of present-day KwaZulu-Natal. This South African state is where most Zulus live today.

Rejected

Do you know how I got my name? I-Shaka means "the parasite" — an unwanted animal that lives and feeds inside someone. My people called me this to insult me. They did not think it was right that my mother gave birth without being married, and they did not want me in their clan.

I've lived in Senzangakona's kraal since my mother became his third wife months after my birth. But he ignores me. The other children tease me for being small and say I am not Senzangakona's son. I am rejected by my people.

Zulu settlements

A kraal is an enclosed settlement containing a central, fenced area for cattle and goats, surrounded by a circle of huts where family members live. The whole kraal is enclosed with a fence of sharpened stakes to keep out wild animals and also enemy people who may want to kill or to steal livestock.

Leaving the Zulus

Today, we were banished from the Zulu kingdom. It is all my fault. I was looking after Senzangakona's sheep as they grazed. It was a hot day and I accidentally dozed off. I woke to see a dog killing one of the sheep. Senzangakona was so angry with me that he told my mother to take me and my younger sister and go.

Like all Zulu children, I was expected to look after livestock while they grazed outside the kraal but also tend to them inside.

Document it!

This book follows Shaka's life from birth to death. But journals don't have to be in order of dates. Your journal could be thematic with sections on different aspects of your life such as music, films, fashion, or pets.

With the Langeni

We are now back living amongst my mother's people, the Langeni. It took one day to walk to their home in the Mhlathuze Valley, around 30 kilometres (20 miles) away. I remember thinking that things would get better for us, but they have got even worse. The Langeni boys are worse than the Zulus. They bully me and tell me I do not belong with them. The only friendly faces I have seen since arriving are my two Zulu aunts who visit often. They are my father's other two wives and always got on well with my mother.

> "Never mind, my Um-lilwane (Little Fire), you have got the isibindi (courage) of a lion and one day you will be the greatest chief in the land."
>
> Nandi, spoken to Shaka

Drought

It is 1802, and we are on the move again. This time it is because of Madlantule, or drought. There have been so many hot months with no rain. Many Langeni cattle have died and people are starving, so we've been sent away. We will go north to stay with my mother's aunt in the Mthethwa chiefdom. Maybe life will be better there.

The grass has turned brown all around and the maize is too dry and hard to eat.

Maize

Southern African people started to grow maize to eat in the 18th century after meeting Portuguese farmers growing it in what is now Mozambique. Maize produces lots of filling food on small areas of land and can be dried easily for storage. But it needs lots of water to grow.

Standing out

At last, I am happy! I like living amongst the Mthethwa. At first, I still got bullied, but not anymore. Why? Because I have grown tall and strong and have discovered that I am very good at Zulu stick fighting. No other teenager of my age can beat me in a bout! Finally, the other boys have started to respect me. They follow me in games and we hunt for wild animals such as leopards. I can't wait until I am old enough to become a Mthethwa soldier. Then I will prove my fighting skills amongst men.

We each have two sticks to fight with, one for hitting and one for defending ourselves.

In the army

The other soldiers call me Nodumehlezi. It means the one who causes the earth to rumble, by making the enemy run away and by leading my soldiers into war. I was 23 when I joined the army and was soon noticed by the Mthethwa chief, Dingiswayo. He saw that I was brave and could lead others. Now, six years later, I am a top commander of his troops.

These modern Zulu men are taking part in a dance festival. With their spears and shields, it is not difficult to imagine how fearsome Zulu warriors must have been.

Dingiswayo

Dingiswayo was leader of the Mthethwa chiefdom, which was made up of several small, independent clans. He created a trained, professional army after learning about how European armies were run. The success of the Mthethwa in battle influenced how other African armies were organized.

Zulu leader

I am now leader of the Zulus! It started with my father Senzangakona's death. I know he did not like me, but I am his eldest son and therefore the rightful heir to the Zulu chiefdom. He must have heard about my leadership skills, but still he chose my brother Sigujana as his successor. Knowing how I felt, Dingiswayo lent me soldiers to challenge Sigujana and his loyal troops for the leadership of the Zulus. There was no other way but to kill Sigujana. Now his troops and all Zulus follow me.

Here I am about to lead my men in battle.

New weapons

We are an army of 400, but not yet the fighting force I want. I have seen in battle how enemies are killed when stabbed with short spears close up, but are more often only injured when hit by long spears thrown from a distance. So I have asked a good blacksmith in a neighbouring clan to make short spears from strong metal with broad, sharp blades. With these new weapons, my soldiers will be invincible.

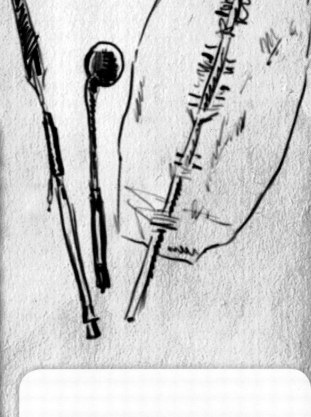

Guns

Zulus mostly fought in close combat using spears in the 18th and 19th centuries, and rarely used guns. Any guns they had were often those seized in battle from other clans. These other clans sometimes traded goods such as animal skins, fresh food, and water for guns from Europeans living in coastal settlements such as Cape Colony (area around present-day Cape Town).

"Shaka called the new stabbing spear iKlwa after the sucking sound it supposedly made when it was withdrawn from the victim's flesh."

Bruce Vandervort, author of a book on wars in Africa, 1998.

New organization

Dingiswayo taught me how to organize an army. I have divided the soldiers up by age and fighting experience into regiments called amabutho. Each amabutho lives in a separate kraal with its own herd of cattle of different skin colour to the others. People can tell which amabutho a man comes from by their distinctive hide shields, headdresses, and ornaments. Soldiers in an amabutho are like brothers and would die for each other in battle.

There can be no finer cattle in the world than our Zulu animals, descendants of the great Nguni cattle of our ancestors.

Cattle

Cattle were very important for Zulus and other clans in southern Africa. They provided meat, milk, leather, horn for ornaments and containers, and dung for fuel. They were also a sign of wealth. Rich, important people had large herds, and clans took herds from other clans they defeated as a sign of military success.

Army life

My amabuthos must train as hard as I did so they are fit and mobile. The soldiers are slow at first, but soon think nothing of marching 80 kilometres (50 miles) a day. Amabuthos can only leave the army when I decide they have given their all — usually when they are past 40 years old. Then I decorate them with a special headring, give them cattle, and allow them to marry.

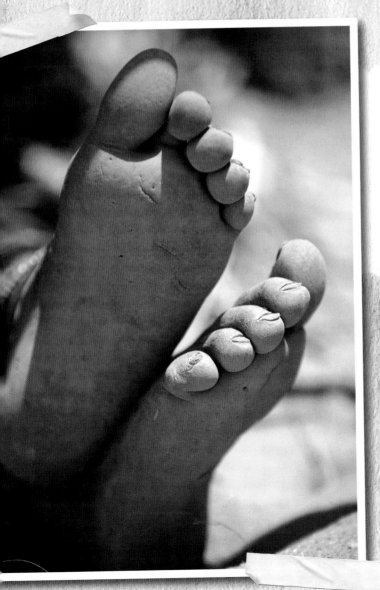

My feet are like leather and I can run over thorny ground for many kilometres. I expect my troops to do the same.

Document it!

Shaka enjoyed being part of a team. Keep a record of what you did with any clubs or other groups and record who was in your teams. Newspaper cuttings and photos are fascinating and will help you remember in the future.

Fighting

A Zulu soldier must be fit, brave, and willing to fight to the death for me and for his amabutho. But we can only win battles if the amabuthos are well organized and fight together. So I have taught them the "bull's horns strategy" that I learnt in the Mthethwe army. The fighting force divides up into four groups who attack, surround, and then destroy the enemy.

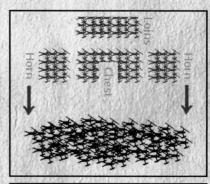

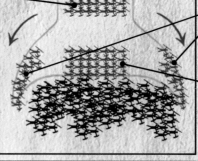

Loins: a group that sits and waits to reinforce our numbers if too many fall

Horns: two groups of younger, faster amabuthos who run around and attack the enemy's sides and rear

Chest: my most experienced amabuthos who charge and fight the enemy head on

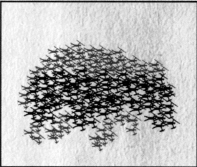

It is a beautiful sight to see my army swarm like biting ants around a fallen locust.

In the heat of battle, I cannot be everywhere and tell all my amabuthos what to do. So I rely on my trusted friend Ngomane and other indunas (officers) to help organize the Zulu forces. The indunas use hand signals to communicate with the soldiers, for example, to tell them where to go. They also keep in constant touch with the soldiers not actually in battle, including my youngest troops, to tell them to bring more weapons or food for the fighting amabuthos.

> *"Strike an enemy once and for all. Let him cease to exist as a tribe or he will live to fly in your throat again."*
>
> Shaka Zulu from *Shaka Zulu: The Rise of the Zulu Empire* (1955) by E.A. Ritter

Ngomane

Ngomane was a trusted induna of Dingiswayo, and leader of the Mthethwa chiefdom. He became friends with Shaka and Nandi when they first moved away from the Langeni clan. They were so close that he helped Shaka become chief of the Zulus and stayed with him as second-in-command.

My kingdom grows

Now is the time to make my Zulu kingdom bigger. We need more grazing land for our cattle and more soldiers for our army. We have started attacking neighbouring clans.

My soldiers love to wash their spears in the blood of our enemies.

Revenge

Last week, I finally took revenge against the Langeni clan, who had so mistreated my mother and me when I was a boy. We marched at night and surrounded the kraal of the Langeni chief. He surrendered, and I had no argument with him. But when we left later the same day, those who had made our lives a misery were dead or dying, and the surviving Langeni had become part of the Zulu chiefdom.

"The slayers will sharpen the ... poles in this cattle-kraal – one for each of you. They will then ... impale you on each of the sharpened poles. There you will stay till you die, and your bodies, or what will be left of them by the birds, will stay there as a testimony to all, what punishment awaits those who slander [mistreat] me and my mother."

Shaka Zulu warning the Langeni of his revenge from *Shaka Zulu: The Rise of the Zulu Empire* (1955) by E.A. Ritter

Document it!

Many quotes by Shaka come from a book written by an Englishman called Erneste Ritter. Ritter had heard the stories of Shaka partly from his Zulu servant, whose father had been one of Shaka's soldiers. The stories were passed down from father to son. Some remembered stories about events in your family may not be completely accurate, but are still important records of past events.

Battling the Ndwandwe

It is 1818, and my kingdom has suddenly grown bigger. My friend and teacher Dingiswayo was murdered by Zwide, chief of the Ndwandwe clan. As his most trusted commander, I took over Dingiswayo's Mthethwe chiefdom and took his army into my Zulu kingdom. We have vowed to smash the Ndwandwe and avenge Dingiswayo's death, even though they have a bigger army.

We will not rest until the earth is soaked in Ndwandwe blood!

Zwide

Zwide was chief of the Ndwandwe from 1805 to 1825. The Ndwandwe attacked the Mthethwe people for years, partly hoping to capture them as slaves for sale to Portuguese traders living on the coast in the north. The traders wanted African slaves to work on sugar plantations in Brazil, where they had a colony.

Gqokli Hill

My heart races at the thought of the Battle of Gqokli Hill. The Zulu army tricked the Ndwandwe into thinking we had a much larger force attacking from one direction by using many decoy oxen and carts without people in them. Then we attacked them from another direction. Zwide was defeated, and now the Ndwandwe people are ruled by the Zulus, too!

Gqokli Hill overlooks the White Umfolozi River.

"Great nation of Zulu, You have shown courage against a superior enemy. The nations that spoke of you with contempt are chilled by your songs. Kings and princes shiver in their little thrones. Enemies flee to hide in the mountain caves."

Shaka, after beating the Ndwandwe

My capital

I have named my capital city KwaBulawayo, which means "at the place of suffering". This name reminds me of my childhood and how my life has changed. KwaBulawayo is a mighty, royal kraal of 1,400 circular huts made from good sticks and grasses. Each has a hard floor of cattle dung and soil. We have many grain pits, because whenever I defeat another clan my soldiers seize supplies of maize and millet grain to help feed my people.

isiZulu

isiZulu is the Zulu language. It is a mixture of the Xhosa language, used originally in southern Africa, and the language used by Nguni people who moved into the area. One way Shaka controlled his kingdom was to make everyone use the same mix of words in one Zulu language. Today, isiZulu is still spoken by around 10 million people. See the "Find out more" section in this book for a website where you can learn isiZulu words.

Document it!

Write about and take photos of where you live for your journal. Your house, street, or town may seem too familiar now, but in future these records will bring back all sorts of memories.

The royal kraal would have looked a
bit like this one in Lesotho.

Zulu women

Zulu women in my kingdom manage their households, while the men get on with fighting. I also need women in my life. My Zulu aunts understand why I would choose one course and not another. So they are the ones who make decisions when I am away. They also make sure soldiers of one clan only marry women of another. You see, clans with mixed blood will not rise up against me.

I cannot understand why other leaders have sons. Dingiswayo was a great leader, but when he was young, he plotted with his brother to take over the Mthethwe from his father. I don't want to be looking over my shoulder for trouble, so I will not get married and I will not have children.

This modern-day Zulu princess is playing an instrument called an ugubhu.

State cattle

I never tire of looking at the Royal Herds. There are so many partly because my aunts took the most desirable young women from important Zulu clans and offered them as brides to wealthy men in other Zulu clans. The men had to give many cattle to the Royal Herds to pay me for the right to marry.

Wealth in Africa

Cattle were a sign of wealth for Zulus, but Europeans were attracted to Africa for other valuable resources. These included slaves to work in mines, and on plantations growing sugar cane in the Americas. The Portuguese first took African slaves in the 15th century. Other valuable African resources in Shaka's time included elephant ivory, copper, and spices such as pepper.

Pepper

Elephant tusks

The crushing

The land is not so good now, so my forces need to spread further to get what we need. Other tribes fear the brutal power of my army. We take young women and men to live with us. But we slaughter older people, as they are no use to us. Some tribes such as the Ndebele have fled, leaving empty lands. We call this Mfecane — the crushing.

Mzilikazi

Mzilikazi was a trusted induna of Shaka, but also a leader of the Ndebele tribe. In 1822, Shaka sent Mzilikazi and his troops to fight a tribe on his behalf. Mzilikazi won, but refused to hand over the spoils of battle to Shaka because he wanted power. He led the Ndebele tribe north, crushing other tribes on the way. After seven years, they settled in an area called Matabeleland, part of present-day Zimbabwe.

The Ndebele were also known as the Matabele people.

New kingdoms

I hear that the Ngwane, Sotho, and Kololo tribes went over the Drakensberg Mountains to the west. The Ndebele are travelling up the Vaal river banks in search of somewhere to build permanent kraals. These new kingdoms may one day grow big, but they will never match the Zulus!

Outside pressures

Some historians believe that Shaka's desire for a bigger kingdom was just one reason for the movement of tribes during the Mfecane. Another reason may have been the presence of slave traders in southern Africa that forced clans to move for safety. Tribes may also have moved to look for better maize farmland due to drought.

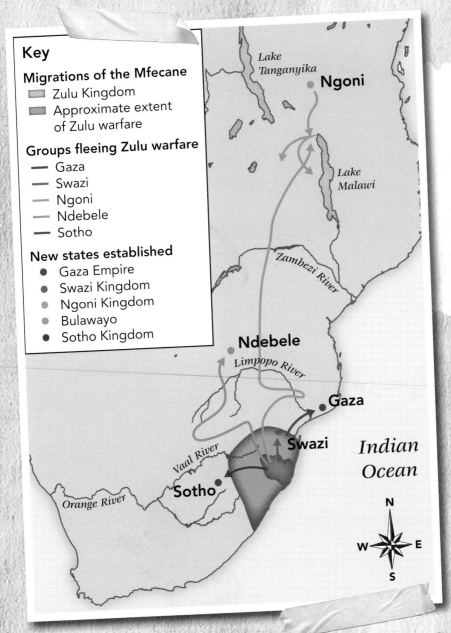

Key

Migrations of the Mfecane
- Zulu Kingdom
- Approximate extent of Zulu warfare

Groups fleeing Zulu warfare
- Gaza
- Swazi
- Ngoni
- Ndebele
- Sotho

New states established
- Gaza Empire
- Swazi Kingdom
- Ngoni Kingdom
- Bulawayo
- Sotho Kingdom

The Mfecane during the 1820s led to several new states and empires forming in southern Africa outside the Zulu kingdom.

Wasteland

Huts are burning and fields lie untended. Hyenas and vultures feed on hundreds of dead bodies. This is what my indunas have told me they have seen again and again in the lands around my kingdom. They have even seen people so hungry that they would eat other people to stay alive. This has happened because tribes scattered by Zulu advances have destroyed villages they have moved through in search of new places to live.

I did not intend to create this wasteland in return for a greater Zulu kingdom.

Unrest

I can feel growing unrest in the Zulu kingdom. There are rumours that some members of my family want a new Zulu leader. They think that the endless battles for new lands are weakening the kingdom. It is not surprising that people whose tribes were pushed from their lands and forced to go hungry at the hands of my troops have a grudge against me. This includes tribes like the Qwabe, who have fled but who once helped me in battle against Zwide and upon whose ancestral lands I built KwaBulawayo.

When tribes moved on, they took as many cattle as they could to start a new life elsewhere.

Document it!

In Shaka's time, wars between tribes were common. When you create your journal, include some information about any wars, conflicts, or political events of the time. This puts the details of your life and times into a historical context.

Changing kingdom

Some weeks ago, a messenger arrived at Kwa Bulawayo saying a great ship called *Antelope* had arrived at Port Natal near by. The white men aboard wanted to meet me. I kept them waiting for a few weeks. But finally, I invited them to my kraal. They arrived on horseback carrying gifts, including new guns, and then ate with me. One man, Henry Fynn, spoke our isiZulu language. He told me about the powerful English king and their hopes for setting up a trading station at Port Natal.

The leader of the men that landed in 1824 was Francis Farewell. He knew the importance of good relations with Shaka in setting up an English settlement.

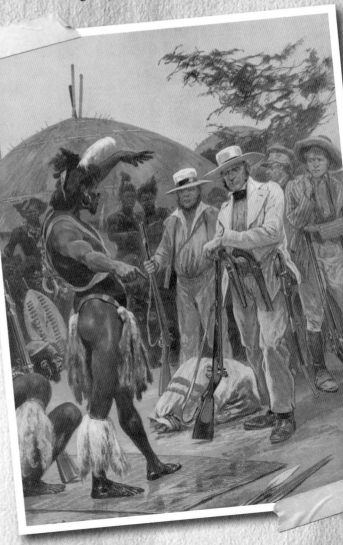

"I hear you have come from umGeorge [King George], is it so? Is he as great a king as I am?"

Shaka to Henry Fynn

My gift of land began a change in my lands. Hundreds of English people moved into the Zulu kingdom.

Gift

Henry Fynn is most interested in our Zulu life and has been staying at my kraal. Just as well, because his medicines saved my life after I was stabbed at a crowded dance by one of Zwide's men. In thanks, I gave him a gift of land around Port Natal. The British said that as Henry Fynn was one of them then that meant the land was owned by King George. So they have their trading station!

British in South Africa

In 1806, the British were fighting the French army, which was led by Napoleon. They took over Cape Colony from Dutch colonists there to stop Napoleon from controlling trade routes to Asia. In 1820, around 4,000 poor British settlers immigrated to live and help defend the Cape from local tribes. Some of the settlers moved to Port Natal – present-day Durban – in May 1824.

Dukuza

We have just finished building a large, new barracks near Port Natal at Dukuza. Seeing my fine Zulu troops every day will remind the British of my power. We can also keep an eye on what they are up to.

Henry Francis Fynn

Henry Fynn was born in 1803 and trained as a surgeon's assistant in London. He moved to Cape Colony and learnt the Xhosa language. Upon moving to Port Natal, he learnt isiZulu and learnt about Zulu culture by living with Shaka and his people. Fynn's diaries and sketches are important records telling us about the Zulu leader and also Nguni history.

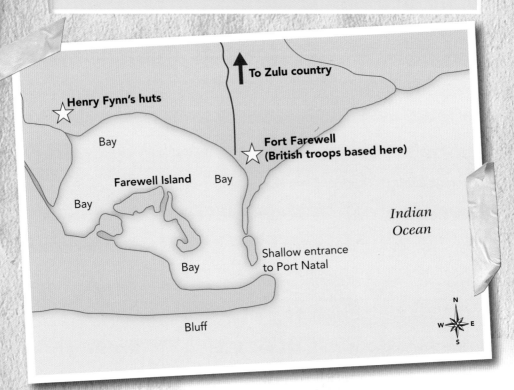

The British could load and unload goods from their ships in the sheltered waters of Port Natal. But they were under the watchful eyes of the Zulus.

We have been trading ivory and skins with the British for metals and fine cloths. As their traders have got richer, more settlers have arrived to get rich, too. Everything is peaceful between our people but who knows what the future holds?

Watching us

Fynn is fascinated by me and my people. He spends hours watching women and children farming, men sharpening their spears, and all kinds of things that happen every day. He writes and draws in books of paper. He looks shocked when I order cowardly soldiers or other people I do not trust to be killed under the killing bush at KwaBulawayo. He thinks I am cruel, but it is only my Zulu way.

"On a mere sign by Shaka ... the pointing of his finger, the victim would be seized by his nearest neighbours; his neck would be twisted and his head and body beaten with sticks."

Henry Fynn, 1824–1836

My people are terrified of me as they would be a powerful god. They will kill on my command and are powerless to refuse me.

35

Death of Nandi

My saddest day has come; my mother, Nandi, died last week. But why are my people not as sad as me? I feel like killing those who do not wail or cry like me, even women about to be mothers themselves. I would be nothing without Nandi, and no mother will ever be as great. I will order no crops to be planted this year. Cattle will be killed and no milk will be drunk. My people's lives should fall apart as mine has.

Nandi's tomb was a grain pit. Her servants were killed and buried alongside her, like any important Zulu.

Document it!

Shaka's grief made him angry and more ruthless than ever. Any death in a family causes confusion and sadness, but it is also an occasion to celebrate someone's life. You can remember your loved ones in your journal. Add photos, create a family tree, and a timeline of their history, too.

Tensions rising

Tensions are rising amongst the Zulus. In 1828, I sent my army south to capture territory near Cape Colony so we could trade with the British there. When they returned, I sent them immediately to fight in the north. Why not? Zulu warriors can take continuous warfare. My aunt and my brother Dingane say nothing, but I have seen them exchange looks. Do they question my leadership?

"I need no bodyguard at all, for even the bravest men who approach me get weak at the knees and their hearts turn to water... They know no other will except that of their King, who is something above, and below, this earth."

Shaka

There is something I do not trust about Dingane, even though he is my brother.

After Shaka

On 22 September 1828, Shaka was murdered. His bodyguard and half-brothers Dingane and Mhlangana stabbed him near his military barracks at Dukuza. As an insult, they left his body in the open for hyenas to eat. But people loyal to Shaka buried his body in a grain pit in the Royal Herd pen.

> *"Hey brother! You kill me, thinking you will rule, but the swallows will do that."*
>
> (By "the swallows", Shaka meant the white people, because they made their houses of mud, as swallows do.)

The Voortrekkers

Voortrekkers were farmers of Dutch origin who escaped the harsh rule of the British at Cape Colony in search of a new life. From the 1830s onwards, they spread outwards through tribal lands, many of which were empty after the Mfecane.

The Voortrekkers arrived by land in the Zulu kingdom after their trip in wagons from the Cape. This was the Great Trek. They proved a formidable fighting force against the Zulus.

These young Zulu people are enjoying a barbecue. Their modern lives are mostly very different from those of people in Shaka's time.

New leader

Shaka had no children, so Dingane became leader of the Zulu nation – but only after executing Mhlangana and his other brothers. Within two years of Shaka's death, the Voortrekkers had arrived in Zulu lands from Cape Colony. This started the first wars between Zulus and white people.

Changes to Zulu land

From the 1840s the British gradually took control of southern Africa from the Voortrekkers and other settlers, especially after large amounts of valuable gold and diamonds were found in the territory in the 1860s. In 1879, the British army attacked the Zulus as they were a threat to British settlers. Shaka's kingdom was broken up and became part of the state of South Africa, ruled at first by the British and more recently by an elected government. Today, the state of KwaZulu-Natal is homeland to the Zulu people who are descendants of Shaka's time.

Timeline

1787   Shaka is born to Nandi and Senzangakona

1793   Nandi and Shaka go to live with the Langeni

1802   Nandi and Shaka leave the Langeni during drought and join the Mthethwa

1809   Dingiswayo becomes leader of the Mthethwa

1810   Shaka becomes a soldier in Dingiswayo's army

1816   Senzangakona dies; after defeating his brother, Shaka becomes chief of the Zulus; he builds his kraal at KwaBulawayo

1817   Mfecane begins

1818   Death of Dingiswayo; Shaka defeats Zwide and his Ndwandwe forces at the battle of Gqokli Hill

1822   Mzilikazi defects from Shaka and leads the Ndebele people from the region

1824   HMS *Antelope* is the first British ship to arrive at Port Natal (present-day Durban); after Fynn saves his life, Shaka grants him possession of land at the port

1827   Nandi dies and the country is forced to go into mourning

1828   Shaka sends his warriors to the borders of Cape Colony and then north of Zulu lands

1828	Shaka is killed by his half-brothers Dingane and Mhlangana on 22 September
1835	Great Trek: Boers leave Cape Colony and occupy new areas of southern Africa
1838	Dingane murders Piet Retief and other Voortrekkers; Dingane and his forces are defeated by the Boers at the Battle of Blood River
1840	After a further defeat, Dingane flees to Swaziland where he is killed; Mpande becomes Zulu ruler
1852	British take control of Cape Town
1867	Large diamond deposits are discovered at Kimberley and the British decide to bring the country into the British Empire
1879	The Zulu army, led by Cetshwayo, defeats the British at Isandlwana but they are later defeated at Ulundi, Natal
1880– 1881	Anglo-Boer War: The Boers rebel against the British, leading to battles between the British army and Voortrekkers and other people of Dutch ancestry in South Africa
1899– 1902	Boer War between British and Boers; Britain wins
1910	South Africa is born as a union of British- and Boer-dominated states

Fact file

Rulers after Shaka

Dingane Under Dingane, the Zulus got into conflict with the British at Port Natal and with the Voortrekkers. In 1838, he executed over 100 Voortrekkers and then attacked their camps, killing 500. The Voortrekkers regrouped and avenged their comrades at the famous Battle of Blood River. Their force of 460 with guns defeated 10,000 Zulus with spears, killing 3,000. Dingane burnt his kraal and fled. Dingane's half-brother Mpande joined the Voortrekkers and helped them defeat Dingane. He was then installed as Zulu king.

Cetshwayo He was the son of Mpande, who revived the Zulu army after Mpande's death in 1872. In 1878, diamonds were discovered in other areas of South Africa and the British decided to take the country. They invaded Zululand and although Cetshwayo beat the British several times, the Zulus could not withstand the superior weapons of the British and were defeated. Cetshwayo was captured and sent to London, where he met Queen Victoria. He was restored to his throne and Zululand became one of 13 chiefdoms established by the British. He died in 1882.

Zulus in the 20th century

Zulus were involved in the Boer War of 1899–1902 working for both the British and the Boers – for example, as trench diggers. In 1910, after the British had won the war, Zululand became part of the Republic of South Africa. In the 1948 elections, the National Party won and started the policy of apartheid. This meant that black people and mixed-race people in the country lost many rights. For example, they could not marry white people, use the same public transport as white people, or live outside areas of the country called homelands, including kwaZulu. Apartheid did not end until 1990. Following democratic elections in 1994, Nelson Mandela became the first black president of the country. KwaZulu then became the state of kwaZulu-Natal.

Write your own journal

What sort of journal would you make to record events from your life? Would it mostly be words or would you illustrate it with sketches and photos? Would you include newspaper cuttings, plane tickets, or anything else that will help you to remember important, happy, or special events? There are two main ways you can create a journal:

On paper

Some journals are created on paper. First decide how big you want your journal to be. You can buy ready-made, bound notebooks or scrapbooks of different sizes. But you can also make your own from folded large sheets of paper with thicker card on the outside. Bind the spine using ribbon or string pushed through holes made with a hole punch.

You could also use a loose-leaf clip folder with loose, punched sheets of paper put in. The advantage of this is that you can add more pages as you create the journal and also different types of pages. For example, there may be plain pages for sketches, envelopes containing tickets, programmes, or other souvenirs, as well as lined pages for neat handwriting.

On screen

Other journals are created on a computer. There are several advantages of on-screen journals over paper ones. For example, you can type in and edit what you have written, scan in photos, and load up digital images onto pages, easily shift images around, and change their sizes. You can also make identical copies of what you have made to give to friends or family. However, you may not always be near a computer to keep this sort of journal up to date, and if there is a power cut or you forget to save, your precious memories could become unavailable, or even lost!

Glossary

amabutho regiment of warriors in Zulu army divided from others by age

apartheid law in South Africa from 1948 to 1990 under which black people were forced to live separately from white people and suffered a variety of inequalities

barracks set of buildings where soldiers live

bull's horns strategy fighting strategy developed by Shaka where groups of soldiers move around the enemy in a shape that resembles a bull's head and horns

Cape Colony area around what is now Cape Town settled by Dutch people in the early 17th century and taken over by the British in the early 19th century

chiefdom group of families led by a chief who normally inherits the role from his father

clan group of families of the same ethnic background

context circumstances and setting that help to make an action, idea, statement, or event easier to understand. For example, Shaka punished the Langeni people in the context of their mistreatment of him and his mother when he was young.

Dingiswayo leader of the Mthethwa chiefdom

grain pit hole for storing dry grain for use later. Grain pits were also used as burial sites by the Zulus.

heir person entitled to the property or the position of someone who has died

hunter-gatherer person who moves around a region to hunt or forage foods from the wild rather than farming in a fixed location

immigrate permanently move to live in a foreign country or region

induna officer in the Zulu army

isiZulu language of the Zulu people

kraal area surrounded by an outer fence, containing huts for a clan or larger group of people in southern Africa. There is an inner fenced area for cattle.

KwaBulawayo Shaka's first capital city

Langeni chiefdom of Nguni people who lived near the Zulus

Mfecane period of movement of chiefdoms and tribes in southern Africa, caused partly by aggression and expansion by the Zulu people

Mthethwa chiefdom of the Nguni tribe that Shaka's mother came from, and amongst whom Shaka lived from his teenage years

Nandi mother of Shaka

Nguni tribe of African people that originated in central Africa and moved southwards in the first millennium BC

Senzangakona father of Shaka and king of the Zulus until his death when Shaka succeeded him

slave person legally owned by another, who is forced to obey and work for them. Many African slaves were taken by European people to do their hard work in mines, growing crops for sale, and in their homes during the 18th and 19th centuries.

successor someone who takes over another person's role after they have gone, or given it up

sugar plantation farm where sugar cane is grown as a crop, harvested, and processed into sugar. In the 17th century, this work was usually carried out by slave labour.

tribe group of people with culture, language, and political organization in common yet who do not necessarily all live in the same place or region

Voortrekker person of Dutch descent living in the Cape Colony in the 19th century, who moved north-east into other parts of southern Africa

Zulu stick fighting sport and martial art that is part of Zulu culture and, in the past, important as training for war. Two people compete, and each person has two sticks and a shield.

Zwide leader of the Nwandwe chiefdom, enemies of the Mthethwa people

Find out more

Books

African Empires (Black History), Dan Lyndon (Franklin Watts, 2010)

Nelson Mandela, Kadir Nelson (HarperCollins, 2013)

Shaka (Jacana Pocket Guides), Dan Wylie (Jacana Media, 2011)

Slavery: From Africa to the Americas (Documenting the Past), Christine Hatt (Evans, 2006)

South Africa (Countries Around the World), Claire Throp (Raintree, 2013)

Websites

www.apartheidmuseum.org/comics
Read an online comic about life under apartheid at the Apartheid Museum website.

www.bbc.co.uk/ahistoryoftheworld/explorerflash/#/culture/60
Explore African history through objects you can see and read about on this fascinating website. You can also look at any other region or type of object by searching the History of the World website.

www.english.emory.edu/Bahri/apart.html
Discover more about the apartheid laws and their impact on life for the majority of South Africans on this website.

www.sahistory.org.za/people/king-shaka-zulu
This website has short, informative biographies of different African leaders, including Shaka Zulu.

www.timeforkids.com/destination/south-africa/native-lingo
Want to hear some isiZulu language being spoken? Visit this website to find out how to say basic phrases such as "hello", "goodbye", and "cool".

www.zulu-culture.co.za/index.php
Learn about all kinds of aspects of Zulu life, from crafts and dancing to food and religion.

Places to visit

British Museum
Great Russell Street
London
WC1B 3DG
www.britishmuseum.org
Want to see a Zulu shield and stabbing spear? These are just two of the 200,000 African objects in the collection of the British Museum.

Apartheid Museum
Corner of Northern Parkway and Gold Reef Roads
Ormonde, Johannesburg
South Africa
www.apartheidmuseum.org
If you ever get the chance to go to South Africa, you could visit the Apartheid Museum. It has many photos, artefacts, and displays about apartheid and 20th-century history of South Africa.

KwaZulu-Natal Museum
237 Jabu Ndlovu Street
Pietermaritzburg
South Africa
www.nmsa.org.za
The KwaZulu-Natal Museum has exhibitions on the history of the state, from earliest people and African and European settlers, to wildlife and Zulu culture.

Index

A RADIOGRAPHIC INDEX

A Radiographic Index

MYER GOLDMAN

MB ChB FRCR DMRD
*Consultant Radiologist, Fazakerley and
Walton Hospitals,
Liverpool*

DAVID COPE

BA FCR DNM
*Superintendent Radiographer,
Walton Hospital,
Liverpool*

Eighth edition

WRIGHT

BRISTOL
1987

Published under the Wright imprint by:
IOP Publishing Limited, Techno House, Redcliffe Way, Bristol BS1 6NX

First Edition, 1961
Second Edition, 1965
Third Edition, 1968
Fourth Edition, 1970
Fifth Edition, 1975
Sixth Edition, 1978
Seventh Edition, 1982
Eighth Edition, 1987

British Library Cataloguing in Publication Data
Goldman, Myer
A radiographic index.——8th ed.
1. Diagnosis, Radioscopic——Dictionaries
I. Title   II. Cape, David, *1930–*
616.07′57′0321   RC78

ISBN 0 7236 0921 7

Typeset by:
BC Typesetting, 51 School Road, Oldland Common, Bristol BS15 6PJ

Printed in Great Britain by:
The Bath Press, Lower Bristol Road, Bath BA2 3BL

Preface to the Eighth Edition

This edition should have a silver cover as it is exactly 25 years since the first edition appeared. And what changes there have been in the practice of diagnostic radiology and radiography in the last quarter century! In 1961 screening was still carried out in near-darkness with the radiologist standing in front of a fluorescent screen. Image intensifiers were just around the corner, however. In that first edition there was, of course, no mention of ultrasound, radioisotope imaging or CT scanning (all of which were first mentioned in the fifth edition in 1975) and these have since been joined by digital subtraction angiography and magnetic resonance imaging (both expanded in this edition) and a host of other new examinations including this time a small section on interventional techniques which open up a new era in which diagnostic radiologists carry out treatment.

The problem is that all these advances have come in a decade in which not only have stringent economies been forced on the NHS, but also when the cost of the new sophisticated machinery is so expensive. Nevertheless, in the four years since our last edition many more hospitals have acquired CT scanners (some by means of charitable appeals involving hard effort by many hospital staff), and now magnetic resonance scanners are beginning to appear sporadically.

This has been a very exciting period to be involved in radiology, but it has given us the problem of how much detail of the older examinations we should leave in. Not every hospital in the UK has a CT scanner by a long chalk, so we have decided to retain many of the conventional techniques, particularly as this book is also used in parts of the world where the more advanced technology is not yet available, at the same time deleting a few which are no longer used, such as presacral pneumography, perirenal air insufflation, pneumoperitoneum and artificial pneumothorax.

We should like to reiterate that all the methods here outlined are a distillation of those used in our own district and that there are alternative techniques in use elsewhere. Even within this group there are variations amongst radiologists in the way they conduct their examinations, e.g. single or double contrast barium meals and enemas, and so on.

We have again revised the whole text, especially the contrast media section which will doubtlessly be out-of-date by the time this appears in print! The 'ten-day rule' section has been dropped in view of recent pronouncements on the subject.

The Preface to the First Edition has been retained for historical interest, and we should like to pay tribute to our former colleague Dr Ronald S. Miller who died at the early age of 35 after the second edition had appeared.

We wish to thank in particular Dr L. Brock for his help with the neuroradiological procedures, Dr Brian Eyes, Dr David Harty and Dr David Meek for their advice on various sections, Dr Geoffrey Smaldon of our publishers, John Wright, for his guidance and encouragement, the subeditors and printers for their painstaking work, and Mrs Ann Cookson for her patience and secretarial assistance.

M.G.
D.C.

Preface to the First Edition

In this pocket-book we have tried to provide in alphabetical form a short practical guide to radiographic positioning and procedures. This is primarily intended for radiographers and student radiographers, but at the same time it is hoped that it might also prove of some value to the trainee radiologist.

Naturally, full details cannot be given in a volume of this size, and our aim has therefore been to give a general synopsis of present-day practice, as carried out in a large general hospital. It must be emphasized, however, that we have made no attempt to be comprehensive, and that there are numerous alternative methods in current use.

We have also included appendices giving a guide to the contrast media in everyday use, a glossary of medical terms, the abbreviations most commonly encountered on X-ray request forms, and a table of average exposure factors.

Our thanks are due to Dr P. H. Whitaker, MD, FFR, DMRE, for writing the foreword and for his continual guidance; and to Dr John Winter, MD, MRad, DMRD, and Dr D. Wallace-Jones, MA, MB, BChir, DMRD, Consultant Radiologists at Walton Hospital, Liverpool, for their constructive criticism and helpful advice throughout.

We also wish to acknowledge the help received with the obstetric section from Dr J. Blair Hartley, MD, FFR, and from Miss A. Stirling Fisher, MSR, and to pay tribute to Miss K. C. Clark, MBE, FSR, author of *Positioning in Radiography*, who kindly read through the draft manuscript and offered us much encouragement.

Finally we should like to thank our wives for their constant enthusiasm; Miss L. Jones for her unfailing patience in typing the manuscript; and our publishers and printers, without whose confidence and assistance this book could not, of course, have been produced.

July, 1960

M.G.
R.S.M.
D.C.

Contents

Note: It is assumed throughout that all exposures are made with an FFD of 100 cm unless stated otherwise in the text.

Radiographic Index

ABDOMEN

  1. Straight. To demonstrate bowel gas, calculi, foreign bodies, abnormal calcification and soft-tissue structures.

    TECHNIQUE. Patient supine with the lower border of the film to the symphysis pubis. Centre to the middle of the film.

  2. Erect and Supine. To demonstrate fluid levels in cases of suspected obstruction.

  Supine. Film as above.

  Erect. As above with patient in erect position. (If there is any question of a perforation, the diaphragm must be included to demonstrate any free air below it. It is usually advisable to take an erect chest film in addition.)

    Note: (1) If the patient is unfit to stand unaided, he may be supported on the table with shoulder-rests under the axillae and immobilizing bands around the abdomen and knees. If this is not possible, the lateral decubitus position should be used. With the table in the horizontal position rotate the patient preferably on to the left side and using a *horizontal beam* and stationary grid, take an AP or PA film.

    Note: (2) A water-soluble oral contrast medium may be used in selected cases (*see* APPENDIX I).

  See also DIAPHRAGM, GALLBLADDER, RENAL TRACT and SUBPHRENIC ABSCESS.

ACETABULUM. *See* HIP JOINT.

ACROMIOCLAVICULAR JOINT. To demonstrate subluxation of the acromioclavicular joint.

  TECHNIQUE. Patient *erect* in the AP position. The body is rotated so as to bring the shoulder of the side under examination against the film, the arm hanging relaxed by the side. Centre just above the head of the humerus. Both sides should be taken for comparison. The gravity effect may be increased by placing a sand-bag in each hand, making sure the shoulders remain relaxed.

    Note: A reduction of about 7 kV is necessary from the corresponding shoulder view.

  See also ACROMION PROCESS, CLAVICLE and SHOULDER JOINT.

ACROMION PROCESS
   1. **Anteroposterior.** Patient erect or supine. Centre just above the head of the humerus.
   2. **Supero-inferior** or **Inferosuperior.** For positioning *see* SHOULDER JOINT.

ADENOIDS. To demonstrate enlarged adenoids encroaching upon the pharynx.
   TECHNIQUE. One film only is necessary. With the head in the true lateral position, centre 5 cm (2 in) above the angle of the jaw.

ADRENAL GLANDS. It has not been possible in the past to demonstrate the adrenal glands with any certainty on plain films of the abdomen unless they are calcified. Methods previously attempted include perirenal air insufflation, selective catheterization of the arteries by means of abdominal aortography and adrenal venography with blood sampling. Nowadays, however, with ultrasonic examination and whole body computerized tomography more accurate visualization is possible.

ALIMENTARY TRACT. *See* ABDOMEN and BARIUM examinations.

ANAL CANAL. To demonstrate imperforate anus in newborn babies.
   TECHNIQUE. A radiopaque marker is placed at the site of the anal 'orifice'. The child is then held upside down for at least 5 min to allow the bowel gas to rise as high as possible in the rectum. Maintaining the position, AP and lateral films are taken.

ANGIOCARDIOGRAPHY. To demonstrate by the injection of contrast medium the blood flow through the heart and great vessels and the function of the ventricles and heart valves. The contrast is injected under pressure through a cardiac catheter into any of the heart chambers, or main vessels. These examinations are normally carried out under local anaesthetic and mild sedation except for young children and nervous adults who may require a general anaesthetic. Strict aseptic precautions must be observed. There must be constant ECG monitoring and facilities for resuscitation immediately available.
   Angiocardiography forms only part of a cardiac catheterization procedure. Prior to the contrast injection the catheter is connected to a pressure measuring system and the pressures

recorded in the chambers of the heart under investigation. In addition, blood samples can be taken to determine the oxygen saturations in the heart chambers and great vessels.

The site of injection, quantity of contrast medium, injection pressure and projections will vary with the condition under investigation and will be decided by the radiologist or cardiologist. Single or biplane ciné film (normally at 25 frames per second but faster, e.g. 90 FPS, for congenital lesions) and video recordings are carried out simultaneously to record the progress of contrast through the heart. The video recording is available for immediate replay to allow the views to be supplemented if required. Rapid sequence cut film can also be used in place of ciné film.

1. **Right Heart.** A radiopaque catheter is introduced by the retrograde technique (*see* AORTOGRAPHY) into the femoral vein or directly into a vein at the elbow following its exposure. Under screen control with image intensification and TV monitoring the catheter is manipulated into the right atrium, through the tricuspid valve into the right ventricle and through the pulmonary valve into the pulmonary arteries. Contrast medium can be injected rapidly at the site of interest. (*See* PULMONARY ARTERIOGRAPHY.)

2. **Left Heart.**
   a. To obtain indirectly the pressure of the left atrium the right heart catheter can be advanced and 'wedged' in a small pulmonary vessel. This is not strictly speaking angiocardiography as no contrast is injected in this position.
   b. If the foramen ovale is patent, or in the presence of an atrial septal defect, the right heart catheter can be passed from right to left atrium.
   c. Trans-septal: A special radiopaque catheter is passed as above from the femoral vein (usually right) into the right atrium. A special long needle is passed up inside the catheter until the sharp curved tip reaches the end of the catheter. The needle/catheter combination is placed against the atrial septum. The septum is then pierced by the needle followed by the catheter. The needle is withdrawn and the catheter left in the left atrium. If required the catheter can be advanced through the mitral valve into the left ventricle.
   d. Retrograde: A long radiopaque catheter is introduced into the femoral artery by the retrograde technique or via an arteriotomy into the brachial artery at the elbow. The catheter is passed retrogradely up the aorta and through

the aortic valve into the left ventricle. Contrast medium can be injected at the root of the aorta (*see* AORTOGRAPHY) or in the left ventricle.

e. Antegrade: Although (*b*) and (*c*) are the methods of introducing catheters into the left atrium this chamber can also be visualized by injecting 50 ml of contrast into the main pulmonary artery and taking delayed ciné film. For this the lateral projection is the most frequently used. This technique is used where it is felt that a 'foreign body' is present in the left atrium. e.g. thrombus or myxoma.

Note: In adults for left or right ventriculography usually 40 ml of contrast medium is injected at a rate of 10 ml/sec but for shunts larger volumes of contrast may be required. To demonstrate left ventricular function and mitral valve function biplane 35° RAO and lateral projections are taken but for visualization of the intraventricular septum the LAO 60° projection is preferable. For right ventricular studies a 20° RAO with 20° cranial tilt is a suitable projection.

3. **Digital Subtraction Angiography.** This technique is now being used particularly in left ventriculography for the assessment of the cardiac indices and wall motion (q.v.):

Note: Echocardiography and nuclear cardiography are largely supplementing invasive techniques especially in children but to a lesser extent in adults where the pressures play an important part of the cardiac assessment. *See* ULTRASOUND IMAGING and RADIO-ISOTOPE IMAGING.

ANGIOPLASTY. *See* INTERVENTIONAL RADIOLOGY.

ANKLE JOINT

1. **Anteroposterior.** Patient supine with the ankle resting on the film. The foot should be as near vertical as possible to avoid superimposition of the calcaneum upon the ankle joint. The leg is rotated inwards a little until the malleoli are equidistant from the film. Centre midway between the malleoli.

2. **Lateral.** The patient is rotated to the affected side, with a sand-bag under the flexed knee, and the ankle resting on the film. A small pad placed under the toes is useful to prevent over-rotation. Centre to the medial malleolus. (It is desirable to include the head of the fifth metatarsal on this view.)

3. **Forced Inversion** (To demonstrate torn lateral ligament). An AP view only is taken with the ankle forcibly inverted. This procedure should only be carried out by the orthopaedic surgeon.

See also SUBTALOID JOINT.

ANTRA. *See* SINUSES.

AORTA. To demonstrate the aortic outline and course.
1. **Abdominal** (Only visible when calcified). Patient lateral on the table. Centre to the lower costal margin.
    Note: An AP straight abdomen (q.v.) may also show gross calcification.
2. **Thoracic.** *See* CHEST and BARIUM SWALLOW.

AORTOGRAPHY
1. **Abdominal.** To demonstrate the abdominal portion of the aorta and its branches. The following method is most widely used at present:
    Retrograde. The patient is placed *supine* over a suitable rapid serial film change device and a control film is taken. The examination may be carried out under either general or local anaesthesia. The radiologist inserts a special needle into one of the femoral arteries in the groin, and passes a flexible guide wire through the needle, which is then removed. He then threads a radiopaque plastic catheter over the wire and manipulates them both upwards via the common iliac artery into the aorta. The guide wire is then removed and the exact position of the catheter checked under screen control with an image intensifier and television monitor. When the position is satisfactory, the radiologist injects 20–30 ml of the contrast medium either manually or with a pressure injector. A rapid succession of films is taken, the exact sequence being decided by the radiologist.
    In some cases, e.g. where there is thought to be an iliac artery block, the following alternative method may be used:
    Direct. A control film should be taken with the patient prone before he is anaesthetized. After being anaesthetized, he is again placed in the *prone* position over a suitable rapid serial film change device. The radiologist inserts a special long needle into the patient's back to the left of the midline below the twelfth rib, and passes it obliquely and forward until it enters the aorta. By means of a plastic connection attached to the needle, a pilot dose of 5 ml of the contrast medium is injected. A film is taken and developed immediately—this will indicate the position of the point of the needle (alternatively, screen control may be used). If satisfactory, 20–30 ml of the contrast medium are injected rapidly and films taken as in the retrograde method.
2. **Thoracic.** To demonstrate the thoracic portion of the aorta

and its branches. The method in common use is the retrograde technique (as above, but using a much longer catheter). *See also* CORONARY ARTERIOGRAPHY.

APPENDIX. *See* BARIUM EXAMINATIONS.

ARTERIAL PORTOGRAPHY. *See* PORTAL VENOGRAPHY.

ARTERIOGRAPHY. *See under* BRACHIAL, CORONARY, FEMORAL and RENAL.

ARTHROGRAPHY. To demonstrate the internal anatomy of a joint by the direct injection of a contrast medium, either fluid or gas (air or CO_2), or both.

TECHNIQUE. In children it is most commonly used in the hip joint in cases of congenital dislocation; and in adults in the knee joint when cartilage damage is suspected. The contrast medium is usually injected under local anaesthesia. Films are then taken in the standard positions for the joint under examination, or under screen control.

ATLANTO-OCCIPITAL ARTICULATION. Remove the patient's dentures, hair clips, etc.

1. **Lateral.** Head and neck in the true lateral position, with the median-sagittal plane parallel to the film and the inter-orbital line perpendicular to the film. The film is placed against the side of the head. Centre 2·5 cm (1 in) below the external auditory meatus.

2. **Oblique.** Patient supine or erect facing the tube with the head in the true AP position, and the median sagittal plane and radiographic base-line perpendicular to the film. Centre to the mid-point of the interorbital line, then rotate the head 45° to each side in turn.

3. **Anteroposterior.** Patient supine or erect facing the tube with the median-sagittal plane perpendicular to the film, and the chin slightly raised until the radiographic base-line is tilted up 10–12° from the perpendicular. Centre to a point 2·5 cm (1 in) below the upper lip in the mid-line. (Before exposing, ask the patient to open his mouth as widely as possible, but make sure that the head does not tilt further back in so doing.)

AXIS. *See* ODONTOID PROCESS.

BARIUM ENEMA (Single contrast). To demonstrate the colon and caecum.

PREPARATION. Adequate clearing of the bowel must be obtained prior to examination, either by enemas, washouts, laxatives or suppositories, or a combination thereof.

TECHNIQUE. A suspension of barium sulphate (500 g to 1200 ml), or one of the proprietary preparations (made up according to instructions), is warmed to body temperature and administered via a rectal catheter under screen control. The examination is carried out by the radiologist who observes the barium-filled colon on the screen and takes films as required, rotating the patient into the optimum positions.

A further film is usually required after evacuation of the enema.

> *Note:* The container is normally not more than 90 cm (36 in) above the table-top in order to avoid undue discomfort to the patient.

BARIUM ENEMA (Double contrast).

Now used by many radiologists routinely as it is particularly useful to demonstrate small lesions, such as polyps, and the mucosal pattern. Single contrast examination is more usual in children.

TECHNIQUE. Approximately 500 ml of one of the barium preparations are introduced into the colon as far as the splenic flexure followed by air which displaces the barium round to the caecum. Films are taken as required by the radiologist including decubitus and/or erect views with overcouch tube.

Some radiologists inject a smooth muscle relaxant (e.g. Buscopan or Glucagon) intravenously before commencing the examination.

An alternative method is to carry out a single contrast barium enema after which the patient evacuates the barium and a routine AE film taken. If there has been a good clearance, a rectal catheter is re-inserted with a Higginson's syringe attached. The bowel is then inflated under screen control and films taken by the radiologist as required.

BARIUM MEAL (Single contrast).

To demonstrate the gastro-intestinal tract.

TECHNIQUE. The patient should not be allowed anything to eat or drink for at least 6 hr prior to the examination.

The patient stands behind the fluorescent screen and drinks 50–80 ml of barium when instructed by the radiologist, who is thus able to examine the oesophagus and the mucosal pattern of the stomach. This is followed by up to 300 ml of dilute barium (1 : 1) for further examination of the stomach and duodenum. Films are taken as required in the optimum positions.

Further films may then be ordered by the radiologist in accordance with the clinical history; for instance, in cases of suspected pyloric stenosis he may wish to have a 6-hr film of the upper abdomen (without the patient having had any food or drink), to assess the gastric emptying rate.

If the small intestine, appendix, or colon is under suspicion, films may be taken at intervals up to 24 hr, or even longer according to the rate of passage of the barium.

BARIUM MEAL (Double contrast). Now used by many radiologists routinely as it is particularly useful to demonstrate the mucosal pattern of the stomach and duodenal cap more clearly and thus detect small lesions at an early stage. Not recommended for children or very ill adults. It may be carried out with or without the injection of a muscle relaxant to produce gastric atony.

TECHNIQUE. In the erect position under screen control a small mouthful of barium is given followed by a gas-producing agent with a further small amount of barium. The patient is then placed supine and is rotated through 360° to coat the gastric mucosa. Films are taken in various positions. Later, additional barium may be given in order to fill the stomach and duodenum as in a conventional barium meal.

BARIUM MEAL (Motor meal). To examine in more detail the terminal ileum and ileocaecal region, including the appendix.

TECHNIQUE. The patient is instructed to take 250 ml of a barium suspension approximately 4 hr prior to the examination. By this time the barium has usually reached the terminal ileum, and screen examination is carried out by the radiologist. If this region has not been reached in 4 hr, further screening will be necessary at 5 or 6 hr, or even at 24 hr.

BARIUM MEAL (Small intestine). This is a difficult region to examine and a number of methods have been evolved. Three in current use are as follows:

1. The patient is given 150–300 ml of a colloidal barium sulphate mixture to drink and films are taken at intervals as determined by the radiologist, usually half-hourly or hourly, depending on the part of the small bowel under investigation. Sometimes a 'hastener' is used to promote rapid passage of the contrast medium.

2. A 100 cm (40 in) polythene tube (which has a radiopaque tip) is passed into the stomach in the ward on the night before the examination. The patient is then encouraged to take sips

of water until midnight (after which nothing further should be taken by mouth), and should lie on the right side. In the majority of cases this will induce the tip of the tube through the pylorus, and a straight film of the abdomen taken early on the morning of the examination will confirm its position. If it lies in the third or fourth part of the duodenum, barium is injected as in the third method.

3. The patient's throat is anaesthetized by means of an amethocaine lozenge. A special polythene tube (containing a finer tube with a radiopaque tip) is passed by the radiologist down the oesophagus into the stomach. Under screen control the outer tube is manipulated until it points towards the pyloric canal. The finer centre tube is now pushed into the canal whence it is carried by peristalsis into the duodenum. When the tip is adjudged to lie at the duodenojejunal junction, a barium solution (30 ml of colloidal barium mixed with 60 ml cold water) is injected rapidly down the inner tube under screen control, followed by water (up to 1200 ml) to advance the barium column. Films are taken by the radiologist during the examination as required.

BARIUM SWALLOW. To demonstrate the pharynx and oesophagus; also indirectly to investigate suspected lesions of the heart and great vessels, and for preoperative assessment in cases of bronchial carcinoma. No preparation is needed but if this examination is requested in cases of suspected hiatus hernia, then the patient should be prepared as for a barium meal (i.e. nothing by mouth for 6 hr beforehand).

TECHNIQUE. The patient stands behind the fluorescent screen and swallows a mouthful of barium paste or fluid barium when instructed by the radiologist, who is thus able to observe its course from the mouth to the stomach. Films are taken as required in the optimum positions.

BILIARY TRACT. *See* CHOLANGIOGRAPHY, CHOLECYSTANGIOGRAPHY, CHOLECYSTOGRAPHY, GALLBLADDER, ULTRASOUND and APPENDIX 4.

BLADDER (Straight). To demonstrate opaque bladder stones and other calcified lesions.

TECHNIQUE.

Anteroposterior. Patient supine. With the tube tilted 20–25° to the feet, centre 5 cm (2 in) above the symphysis pubis, the central ray to the middle of the film. If a stone is suspected on this view, an erect film of the same area should be taken.

See also CYSTOGRAPHY, INTRAVENOUS UROGRAPHY and URINARY
TRACT.

BRACHIAL ARTERIOGRAPHY.
To demonstrate the brachial artery and its branches.

TECHNIQUE. The method generally used nowadays is by catheterization via the femoral artery, the long catheter being positioned in the appropriate subclavian artery under screen control. *See* AORTOGRAPHY.

BRONCHOGRAPHY.
To outline the bronchial tree with a contrast medium, especially to reveal blocks and bronchiectasis.

TECHNIQUE. Three methods are in common use:

1. **Oral.** The patient's throat is anaesthetized by giving him an amethocaine lozenge to suck, after which the throat is sprayed with a surface anaesthetic. The contrast medium (20 ml) is then introduced over the back of the tongue using a curved cannula and syringe, following which the patient is placed in various positions in order to fill the different divisions of the bronchi. This may be carried out under screen control.

   Postero-anterior, oblique and lateral films are taken.

   For positioning, *see* CHEST.

   Note: For the oblique views rotate the patient only 45°. To demonstrate the right bronchial tree, take a left anterior oblique film; and for the left, a right anterior oblique.

2. **Cricothyroid.** In this method the medium is introduced directly via a needle into the trachea through the crico-thyroid membrane. The overlying skin and soft tissues are anaesthetized using local anaesthetic. A special wide-bore needle is then used to introduce the contrast medium, following which the patient is positioned as above.

3. **Bronchoscopic.** Following examination with a flexible bronchoscope, contrast medium is instilled under screen control directly into the bronchus of the long segment(s) under investigation.

CAECUM.
See BARIUM EXAMINATIONS.

CALCANEUM (Os calcis).

1. **Lateral.** Position as for a lateral ankle; centre 2·5 cm (1 in) below and 2·5 cm (1 in) behind the medial malleolus.

2. **Axial.** There are many variations of this position, but this is the one most commonly used:

Patient sitting on the table with legs extended, the ankle in the AP position, and the foot dorsiflexed. A bandage is passed around the foot and held by the patient, to maintain dorsiflexion. Centre to the heel (or between the heels if both sides are being examined), with the tube angled at 30° relative to the sole of the foot.

3. Oblique. This view is usually taken to demonstrate the subtaloid joint (q.v.).

CALCIFIED ARTERIES. To demonstrate calcification in the wall of the particular arteries under investigation, usually in the legs.

TECHNIQUE. The films will have to be slightly under-penetrated to demonstrate minor degrees of calcification adequately.

1. Thighs—Anteroposterior. Patient supine, with the upper border of the film placed level with the hip joint, legs extended and feet externally rotated. Centre to the middle of the film. Exposure is about half that for a hip.

2. Legs—Lateral. With the patient turned on to each side alternately, place the film so that its upper border is 5·0–7·5 cm (2–3 in) above the knee joint. (This will enable calcification in the popliteal artery to be demonstrated.) Centre to the middle of the film.

3. Feet–Lateral. With the patient lying on the side under examination, place the film so that the whole of the foot and as much of the lower leg as possible are included. Centre to the middle of the film.

See also AORTA and XEROGRAPHY.

CAPITATE. *See* WRIST JOINT.

CARDIO-ANGIOGRAPHY. *See* ANGIOCARDIOGRAPHY.

CARPAL TUNNEL. *See* WRIST JOINT.

CARPUS (Carpal bones). *See* WRIST JOINT.

CEREBRAL ANGIOGRAPHY.
1. Carotid Angiography. To outline the circulation in the cerebral hemispheres especially the anterior and middle cerebral vessels by injecting a contrast medium. In this way lesions of the vessels, e.g. aneurysms, arteriovenous malformations, or narrowings due to atheroma, or displacements of the vessels caused by, e.g tumours or abscesses, may be seen.

TECHNIQUE. Local or general anaesthesia may be used. The latter is essential for children or uncooperative patients.

> **Direct puncture** has largely been replaced by indirect catheterization, though the direct method is still very useful, particularly if the examination is to be confined to one artery, or if the patient is old. Needles have been largely replaced by cannulae made of plastic or metal. The cannulae are introduced on a removable stilette. When the artery has been punctured, the stilette is replaced by a short flexible guide wire which is used to advance the cannula into the internal (or sometimes the external) carotid artery. The cannula is connected via transparent tubing to a saline-filled syringe which is used to flush it through to prevent formation of blood clots.

> **Indirect catheterization** is carried out by passing a shaped catheter about a metre long, on a guide wire retrogradely up the aorta from the femoral artery, or occasionally from the axillary artery. Using fluoroscopy, which is essential, the catheter may be further advanced into the brachiocephalic (innominate) artery and thence into the right carotid artery, or into the left carotid artery.

> Exposures in both lateral and AP projections are necessary, and it is usual to take a series of films. Eight or more are used in each projection, and a rapid film changer is needed. The AP series is usually taken with the tube tilted 25° towards the feet. Aneurysms of the anterior and middle cerebral arteries are often more clearly seen in oblique or perorbital views in which it may be preferable to take single films with a grid cassette.

2. **Vertebral Angiography.** To outline in particular the posterior cerebral and cerebellar circulation by the injection of contrast medium into one of the vertebral arteries.

> TECHNIQUE. Direct puncture of a vertebral artery in its cervical portion under a general anaesthetic is rarely carried out nowadays, and indirect methods are generally used. These involve either the injection of contrast medium into a vertebral artery by retrograde catheterization via a femoral or axillary artery, as in AORTOGRAPHY and CAROTID ANGIOGRAPHY (q.v.), or Retrograde Brachial Angiography, carried out by puncturing the brachial artery in the antecubital fossa, and using a pressure injector, forcing sufficient contrast medium upwards against the natural blood flow to fill the vertebral and carotid arteries on the right, or the vertebral artery on the left.

CERVICAL RIBS.   To demonstrate supernumerary ribs arising from C.7.

TECHNIQUE

> **Anteroposterior.**   Patient supine or erect. Centre 2·5 cm (1 in) above the sternal notch, with the tube tilted 10° towards the head.
>
> In addition, an apical view of the chest may demonstrate cervical ribs.

CERVICAL VERTEBRAE.   Remove the patient's dentures, hair-clips, etc.

1. **Anteroposterior (C.1–C.3).**   Patient supine or erect facing the tube, with the median-sagittal plane perpendicular to the film and the chin raised slightly until the radiographic baseline is tilted up 10–12° from the perpendicular. Centre to a point 2·5 cm (1 in) below the upper lip in the mid-line. (Before exposing, ask the patient to open his mouth as widely as possible, but make sure that the head does not tilt further back in so doing.)

2. **Anteroposterior (C.3–C.7).**   Patient supine or erect facing the tube, with the chin raised until the peripheral ray will superimpose the symphysis menti over the occiput. Place the film so that the lower border of the mandible will be projected just below the upper border of the film. Centre to the middle of the film, with the tube tilted 5–10° to the head.

3. **Anteroposterior (C.1–C.7).**   Position as in 2 above, but move the film upwards to include all the cervical vertebrae. The patient is instructed to open and close his mouth during the exposure, which is made with a low milliamperage. The exposure time should be between 3 and 5 sec.

4. **Lateral (C.1–C.7).**   Patient erect with the shoulder resting on the lower border of the film in the erect cassette-holder, and the chin slightly raised. The hands are then clasped behind the back and the shoulders pulled back as far as possible. Centre to the angle of the jaw. (180 cm FFD.)

5. **Posterior Oblique (C.1–C.7).**   Patient erect facing the tube. The body is then rotated 45° to either side in turn. The head is then rotated further until it is in the true lateral position, and the chin is raised so that the mandible is not superimposed on the spine. Centre to the middle of the neck 5 cm (2 in) below the level of the angle of the mandible, with the tube tilted 15° towards the head. (*Note:* this view demonstrates the intervertebral foramina of the side *away* from the film. It may be helpful to include both R. and L.

markers on each film, in order to avoid confusion.) (180 cm FFD.)

See also ATLANTO-OCCIPITAL ARTICULATION and ODONTOID PROCESS.

CHEST. To demonstrate pulmonary pathology and the cardiac outline. (All views at 150 cm FFD.)

1. **Postero-anterior.** Patient erect in PA position, the upper border of the film adjusted so that the apices of the chest will be included on the film. The backs of the hands are placed on the hips and the shoulders and arms rotated as far forward as possible without raising the shoulders. (This is to project the scapulae away from the lung fields.) Centre to the fifth thoracic vertebra. The film must be taken in INSPIRATION.

2. **Lateral.** Patient erect with the side under examination against the film, hands on head with the elbows close together in front and raised as high as possible. Centre through the axilla at the level of the fifth thoracic vertebra.

3. **Right Anterior Oblique.** Patient erect, as for PA chest. The LEFT hand is placed on the head, and the patient rotated left side away from the film until the body is approximately 60° to it. Centre to the level of the fifth thoracic vertebra.

4. **Left Anterior Oblique.** As for right anterior oblique but the patient is rotated right side away from the film, until the body is approximately 70° to it.

   Note: It will be seen that the position is defined by that side of the body in contact with the film, and this holds true for all oblique views.

5. **Anteroposterior for Apices (Apical view).** Patient erect with his back to the film and about 30 cm (12 in) in front of it. He then bends backwards until his shoulders rest on the film, whereupon his arms are raised and hands turned out to separate the scapulae as far as possible. Centre to the midline 7·5 cm (3 in) below the line of the clavicles.

   Note: This view, often incorrectly referred to as the 'lordotic' view, is used to project the clavicles above the apices of the lungs, and so enable small lesions there to be demonstrated with greater clarity.

6. **Lordotic.** This view is only used to demonstrate right middle lobe collapse or interlobular pleurisy on the right side. Patient erect as for PA chest. He then grasps the film-support and bends backwards from the waist, approximately 30°. Centre to the level of the fifth thoracic vertebra.

   Note: Although all chest films are normally taken in INSPIRATION, in cases of suspected spontaneous pneumothorax, a PA film should also be taken in EXPIRATION, as sometimes the lesion may be demonstrated on this view when the ordinary film appears normal.

CHOLANGIOGRAPHY (Choledochography). To demonstrate the hepatic and common bile ducts by the injection of a contrast medium during and following operation with particular reference to patency and retained calculi.

1. **Operative.** At open operation fluid contrast medium is introduced directly into the common bile duct. Films are taken with the patient still on the operating table.

2. **Postoperative.** The contrast medium is introduced into the 'T' tube which was inserted into the common bile duct by the surgeon at operation. Radiographs are taken under screen control. It is usual to perform this examination some 10 days after surgery.

CHOLANGIOGRAPHY (Percutaneous Transhepatic). To visualize the biliary tract by the injection of a contrast medium directly through the lateral abdominal wall into one of the intrahepatic bile ducts via a thin flexible needle, under local anaesthesia. This method is used in patients with obstructive jaundice.

CHOLECYSTANGIOGRAPHY (Intravenous). This procedure is used mainly to outline the duct system, particularly in a patient whose gallbladder has been removed. (If available, ERCP is the examination of choice.)

TECHNIQUE. The patient is prepared as for the oral method; 30 ml of the contrast medium are injected intravenously and films are taken after 15–20 min and at subsequent intervals up to 2 hours. Alternatively, 100 ml may be given of half-strength solution by slow infusion over not less than 30 min. If the gallbladder is present and concentrates the medium, a fatty meal may then be given and a film taken 15–20 min later.

Films are taken as for gallbladder (straight).

If the duct system is obscured by bowel contents, a narrow-angle tomographic cut (at about 11–13 cm, depending on the size of the patient) may give more satisfactory visualization.

CHOLECYSTOGRAPHY (Oral). To demonstrate the gall-bladder, and assess its function. (This is sometimes known as Graham's examination.)

Note: In many departments ultrasound examination is now the initial method of choice.

TECHNIQUE. A straight film of the gallbladder area is taken on the day before the examination. The evening meal should contain no fatty or fried foods. At 9 p.m. the contrast medium is taken with water, after which nothing more should be eaten, but water may be drunk until midnight. (In some departments a further quantity of contrast medium is given at 6 a.m. the following morning.) At 9 a.m. films of the gallbladder area are taken in the erect and prone positions. If at this stage the gallbladder is outlined, a meal is given containing a high fat content (e.g. egg and milk) or a standardized fatty-meal preparation and this is followed 30–60 min later by a further film to assess gallbladder contraction.

If no concentration of the medium is observed on the first film the examination may be repeated, a further dose being taken on the same evening.

If the gallbladder is outlined but is partially obscured by bowel gas, a further film with the patient supine, or a narrow-angle tomographic cut, may give more satisfactory visualization.

Note: The latest contrast media often outline the cystic and common bile-ducts as well as the gallbladder (i.e. oral cholecystangiography).

CISTERNOGRAPHY. To show the C.S.F.-containing spaces at the base of the brain, and any abnormalities caused by, e.g. tumours of the pituitary gland, optic nerves or hypothalamus.

TECHNIQUE. A non-ionic contrast medium is injected into the subarachnoid space, usually by the lumbar route, and the patient, lying prone, is gently tipped head down while fluoroscopy is used to monitor the flow of contrast medium. X-rays are then taken, mainly lateral views with tomography, or the patient is transferred to the CT scanner for the remainder of the examination. *See* COMPUTERIZED TOMOGRAPHY.

CLAVICLE. It is preferable to take the films in the PA position but if this is not possible owing to injury, an AP film is usually satisfactory.

1. **Postero-anterior.** With the patient either prone or erect, rotate the body 10–15° until the clavicle of the affected side is against the film. Centre over the middle of the clavicle.
2. **Anteroposterior.** Patient supine or erect with the shoulder

of the affected side against the film. Centre to the middle of the clavicle.

3. **Inferosuperior.** This view is useful to show the amount of displacement of the fragments of a fracture. With the patient supine, the film is supported against the upper border of the shoulder by means of sand-bags. Centre to the middle of the clavicle, the central ray being directed at 45° to the horizontal, making sure that the whole length of the clavicle will be projected on to the film (this will mean pressing the film well into the patient's neck).

See also ACROMIOCLAVICULAR JOINT and STERNOCLAVICULAR JOINT.

CLINOID PROCESSES. *See* PITUITARY FOSSA.

COCCYX

TECHNIQUE. The coccyx may be difficult to demonstrate in the AP position, owing to faecal matter and gas in the rectum. If this is so, the patient will have to be prepared for the examination by means of a rectal wash-out.

1. **Anteroposterior.** With the patient supine, centre to the midline, the central ray being angled 10–15° to the feet and directed about 2·5 cm (1 in) above the symphysis pubis.

2. **Lateral.** With the patient lateral, centre to the coccyx. This is easily felt between the buttocks. Care should be taken to ensure that in this position the coccyx is over the midline of the table.

COLON. *See* BARIUM EXAMINATIONS.

COMPUTERIZED TOMOGRAPHY (CT) IMAGING. This is a revolutionary method of tomography, developed by Sir Godfrey Hounsfield of EMI in 1969–71. It combines an automated X-ray scanning procedure with computerized image processing to provide outstandingly useful diagnostic pictures of the head and body. The method was introduced originally as a brain scanner, but the principle has been extended to produce machines capable of scanning any part of the body, including the head.

1. **Head.** The scanner builds up a picture of the head as a series of 'slices'. Originally the machine used a narrow collimated X-ray beam and a single sodium iodide crystal with an associated photo-multiplier. The beam was made to traverse the head while the detector system took hundreds of readings of the strength of the X-ray beam both entering and leaving the head, thus measuring its absorption in the tissues.

The beam and detectors were then rotated, and the process repeated. The first machines rotated through 1° at a time, for a total of 180°, and took 4–5 min. Modern scanners use many more detectors, sometimes fixed right round the circumference, or in others, in an arc opposite the X-ray tube, but rotating with it. Scanning times have been cut to less than 2 sec in the very fastest machines, by eliminating the transverse motion in favour of rotation only. Different detectors have also been used, including caesium iodide and tubes of xenon gas.

The readings obtained by the detectors are all fed into a computer which calculates the individual absorption values of thousands of small blocks of tissue which are the component parts of a 'slice'. Different absorption values are displayed on a T.V. monitor in different shades, ranging from white, through grey, to black. The picture so obtained shows a cross-section of the head, in which both normal structures (e.g. ventricles) and abnormal ones (e.g. tumours, abscesses, haematomas) can be distinguished. A photographic record is made from the T.V. screen; the patient is moved a small distance, and the process is repeated, but this time obviously at a different level. The 'slice' thickness is usually 1 cm but it can be varied as required. About 10–12 'slices' are usually sufficient to display the head from the base of the skull to the vertex. As the scanning plane is vertical, with the patient lying supine, the 'slices' are transverse. The patient is usually positioned so that the 'slices' are obtained parallel to the radiographic base-line (q.v.), but other positions are used, particularly the prone position with extended neck to obtain coronal views.

From an early date, it was clear that this new method was applicable, not only to the brain, but also to the structures of the head in general, including orbits, pharynx, sinuses, auditory canals and middle ear. The latest machines allow even the auditory ossicles to be seen.

Contrast Enhancement. Takes place when iodine-containing contrast media are injected intravenously. If the patient is scanned within a period varying from a few minutes to two hours, some normal structures (blood vessels, falx cerebri and tentorium cerebelli) and many abnormal tissues (e.g. tumours, infarcts, aneurysms, abscesses) show a higher density due to a selective increase in iodine concentration within them. This phenomenon can be extremely helpful in diagnosis. Direct injection into the CSF of a non-ionic contrast medium which is then allowed to flow into the CSF space in the head, is also a diagnostic aid, and is known as 'Cisternography' (q.v.). Air is used similarly to investigate patency of the internal auditory canal.

CT head scanning gives a radiation dose which is about the same as that from a single skull X-ray. This is a great deal less than that of a cerebral angiogram or air encephalogram, and the procedure is far less upsetting to the patient than either.

2. Body. The scanner operates on exactly the same principles as the head scanner, but clearly needs a larger aperture for the patient, and short scanning times are required because of respiratory and bowel movements. Efforts have been made to obtain better scans of the heart, by 'pulsing' the X-ray beam at the same moment in successive cardiac cycles (using the ECG).

Contrast media are also used in body scanning. Barium in ordinary concentrations is much too dense and ruins the pictures, but may be used in a much lower concentration. Dilute solutions of iodine contrast media may be swallowed, to opacify the gut, or they may be instilled into the bladder. Blood vessels are displayed, exactly as in the head, after intravenous injection or drip.

Most recent scanners have the ability to produce a picture rather like a conventional AP or lateral radiograph, by moving the patient past the X-ray tube and detectors, which are kept stationary. The picture so obtained is very useful for determining the exact anatomical position at which a CT 'slice' is to be taken.

Body scanners have a particularly valuable role in assessing the spread of malignant disease in the chest and abdominal cavities, particularly in the para-aortic and retroperitoneal regions, in the mediastinum, and in distinguishing cysts from tumours in the liver, kidneys and pancreas if ultrasound examination is equivocal. Radiotherapy planning is also made more accurate by CT scanning.

CONDYLE OF MANDIBLE. *See* MANDIBLE.

CORACOID PROCESS. *See* SCAPULA.

CORONARY ARTERIOGRAPHY. To demonstrate the anatomy of the coronary circulation. Catheters, specifically shaped for the left and right coronary orifices, are inserted into the femoral artery using the retrograde technique (*see* AORTOGRAPHY) or a single shaped catheter suitable for both coronary arteries is inserted into the brachial artery above the elbow by an arteriotomy and passed retrogradely to the root of the aorta, and then manipulated under screen control into the opening of the appropriate coronary artery. Small injections of contrast medium are made in various projections and its course through the coronary circulation recorded usually by means of ciné film (at 25 frames per sec) and simultaneously recorded on videotape for immediate replay to allow the views to be supplemented if required.

The normal routine views for the left coronary artery are RAO 35°; LAO 60° and Left Lateral. These can be supplemented by additional oblique views with or without cranial or caudal angulation. For the right coronary artery the same views are used but the supplementary views are seldom if ever required. A magnification technique is usually used.

Digital Subtraction Angiography is now being used to visualise better the coronary arteries and assess the degree of stenosis.

The same precautions as for ANGIOCARDIOGRAPHY (q.v.) must be observed.

CRIBRIFORM PLATE. To demonstrate fractures in the cribriform plate region of the ethmoid bones.

Postero-anterior Oblique. Patient erect or prone, with the head in the true PA position. Rotate the head towards the side being examined until the median-sagittal plane is 40° to the perpendicular. Tilt the chin up until the radiographic baseline is 30° to the perpendicular. Centre through the orbit in contact with the film, with the tube angled 10° towards the feet. Stereoscopic views are recommended.

CUBOID. *See* FOOT.

CUNEIFORM. *See* FOOT.

CYSTOGRAPHY. To demonstrate the bladder outline and ureteric reflux.

TECHNIQUE. The bladder is catheterized and any urine allowed to drain off. About 150 ml of diluted contrast medium are then introduced via the catheter and films are taken in the AP and oblique positions.

1. **Anteroposterior.** Patient supine. Centre to the midline 5 cm (2 in) above the symphysis pubis with the tube tilted 25° to the feet (a film taken with the patient straining may demonstrate ureteric reflux).

2. **Oblique.** From the AP position the patient is rotated

approx. 50° to either side in turn. Centre just medial to the anterior superior iliac spine away from the film, with the tube vertical.

Note: To detect bladder tumours a double contrast technique with air or gas insufflation is sometimes used.

CYSTO-URETHROGRAPHY (Female).   To demonstrate defects in bladder mechanisms, in particular stress incontinence.

TECHNIQUE.   The bladder is catheterized and any urine present drained off. About 150 ml of diluted contrast medium are then introduced via the catheter. (This may be followed by 20 ml of more dense or oily medium to outline the base of the bladder and urethral catheter in situ.) The patient is then seated upon a special chair against an upright Potter-Bucky in the lateral position.

Films are taken: (1) At ease; (2) Straining as if to micturate; (3) During micturition. Further information may be given by an AP film during micturition with the patient seated, knees apart.

CYSTO-URETHROGRAPHY   (Male).   To demonstrate the urethra and bladder neck.

TECHNIQUE.   With the patient supine on the X-ray table, a special penile clamp with a rubber nozzle is placed in position, attached to which is a metal connecting tube and syringe. About 150 ml of diluted contrast medium are then introduced, and this may be followed by 20 ml of more dense or oily medium. As the last few drops are being injected, AP and oblique views are taken. Finally, a film is taken during micturition (it may be found necessary for the patient to stand for this).

Note: If it is desired only to outline the urethra, it will not be necessary first to fill the bladder with the more dilute medium.

DACRYOCYSTOGRAPHY.   To   demonstrate   the   lacrimal ducts.

TECHNIQUE.   The conjunctiva is anaesthetized with local anaesthetic drops. The lacrimal punctum in the lower eyelid is dilated, then a fine cannula inserted. This is attached to a syringe containing contrast medium which can thus be injected into the lacrimal duct. A few drops of the medium may be brushed on to the lash margins to outline the lids on the subsequent radiographs.

Films are taken: (1) Preliminary: Mento-occipital and

lateral views; (2) Immediately following injection; (3) 5–10 min after injection.

DIAPHRAGM. To demonstrate the position and movement of the diaphragm. It is usual to screen these patients, but an adequate assessment of diaphragmatic movement can be made radiographically. These views are also of importance in demonstrating free air under the diaphragm (in cases of suspected perforation).

TECHNIQUE

1. **Postero-anterior.** With the patient erect as for a chest film, the film is placed transversely, the lower border level with the lower costal margin. Centre to the middle of the film.

2. **Lateral.** Patient erect in the lateral position. The upper border of the film is placed at the level of the axillae. Centre to the middle of the film.

3. **Double Diaphragm View.** Patient in PA position as above. The first exposure is made on full expiration giving a normal chest exposure. The second exposure on the same film is made on full inspiration, giving half the previous exposure. This view will demonstrate the full range of movement of the diaphragm on the one film. (150 cm FFD.)

   Note: To demonstrate free air under the diaphragm when the patient is very ill and is unable to stand, the following views may be useful: (100 cm FFD.)

   A. **Anteroposterior Decubitus.** Patient supine with the film vertical against the side of the abdomen. The central ray is directed horizontally at the level of the diaphragm.

   B. **Lateral Decubitus.** Patient in the lateral position on the table with a film and stationary grid vertical against the upper abdomen. Centre to L.1, the central ray being directed horizontally.

See also ABDOMEN (Straight) and SUBPHRENIC ABSCESS.

DIGITAL SUBTRACTION ANGIOGRAPHY (DSA) (also known as Digital Vascular Imaging, DVI). This relatively new technique originally promised a revolution in the examination of the vascular system by permitting angiography without the use of catheters, simply by the IV injection of contrast medium combined with sophisticated electronic and computer technology using real-time image subtraction and enhancement. However, radiologists who practise this method have found that more accurate diagnosis can be obtained by the insertion of venous or even arterial catheters so as to be able to introduce the contrast medium more closely to the organ under examination.

TECHNIQUE

1. **Intravenous.** The contrast medium is introduced into an antecubital vein or by catheter into the superior vena cava or right atrium. By correct timing it is possible to obtain views of the artery under investigation but the quality of the images is not as good as conventional arteriography, and there is the problem of overlap as all arteries are filled simultaneously. It is now clear that IV angiography is particularly valuable as a 'screening' method and can be carried out on outpatients.

2. **Intra-arterial.** This method has all the advantages of conventional angiography in visualising a chosen artery without overlap and has the additional advantage of producing instant pictures. Also, finer catheters can be used with smaller doses of contrast medium, hence there is less discomfort and greater safety.

A disadvantage of both methods lies in their sensitivity to patient movement, especially in the thorax due to respiratory and cardiac movement. Basically, an image intensifier and T.V. camera are centred over the region under examination and digital readouts obtained before and after the injection of the contrast medium. The computer subtracts one set of images from the other (hence the name). The resulting pictures showing only the appropriate arteries are immediately available for viewing on a T.V. monitor and are stored on video disc or tape for future recall.

DISCOGRAPHY. To demonstrate lumbar intervertebral disks by the injection of 0·5–1 ml of contrast medium directly into them through a fine needle inserted via a lumbar puncture needle under screen control. Films are taken in the AP, lateral and oblique projections. This is often carried out prior to chemonucleolysis.

DORSAL VERTEBRAE. *See* THORACIC VERTEBRAE.

DORSILUMBAR JUNCTION. *See* THORACOLUMBAR JUNCTION.

DORSUM SELLAE. *See* PITUITARY FOSSA.

DUODENUM. *See* BARIUM MEAL.

EAR. *See* INTERNAL AUDITORY MEATUS, MASTOIDS and PETROUS TEMPORAL BONE.

ECHOCARDIOGRAPHY. *See* ULTRASOUND IMAGING.

ELBOW JOINT

1. **Anteroposterior.** Patient seated or kneeling at the end of the table, with the arm extended and rotated so that the whole arm and the back of the hand are flat on the table. Centre 2·5 cm (1 in) below the midpoint of the epicondyles. If the patient cannot straighten the arm because of injury, two AP views should be taken, one with the forearm in contact with the film, the other with the humerus in contact. (If the degree of flexion is not excessive one film may be taken with the arm adjusted so that the humerus and the forearm are at equal angles to the film.)

   Note: Where the head of the radius is suspect, it may be of advantage to take the AP view with the arm rotated further outwards, as this will separate the upper end of the radius from the ulna.

2. **Anteroposterior Flexed.** Where there is extreme flexion the humerus should be rested on the film, and the central ray is directed to the elbow joint, the tube being angled 10–15° towards the shoulder.

   Note: In this position the radius and ulna are superimposed on the humerus, but a good guide can be obtained to the position of the bony fragments in the case of gross injury.

3. **Lateral.** Patient seated or kneeling as for AP view, with the elbow and wrist in the true lateral position, the humerus and forearm resting on the table and the elbow flexed to about 90°. Centre to the lateral epicondyle.

4. **Supero-inferior (for ulnar groove).** Patient seated with his back to the table, the elbow flexed and the forearm resting on the edge of the table. (This is the natural position of 'resting on one's elbow'.) The humerus is adjusted 25–30° to the vertical. Centre to the ulnar groove which is just lateral to the medial epicondyle.

5. **Anteroposterior (for head of radius).** An additional view can be taken to demonstrate the articular surface of the head of the radius. With the arm slightly flexed, the point of the elbow is rested on the film and the arm adjusted to make an angle of approximately 30° to the film. Centre to the crease of the elbow.

EMBOLIZATION. *See* INTERVENTIONAL RADIOLOGY.

ENCEPHALOGRAPHY. To demonstrate the ventricular and cisternal systems of the brain by the injection of a gas (air or oxygen) into the lumbar subarachnoid space, or directly into the cisterna magna.

Note: With the introduction of computerized tomography this examination, which is unpleasant for the patient, is now rarely performed. We are, however, retaining the details for reference.

TECHNIQUE

1. **The Lumbar Route** is most commonly used. This is usually carried out with a local anaesthetic after suitable pre-medication (though a general anaesthetic may be used for children and excitable adults).

   The patient sits or is supported upright in front of a skull unit or vertical Potter-Bucky with his forehead against it, and the head slightly flexed. A lumbar puncture is performed and a few drops of CSF allowed to escape. Then 5 ml of the gas are injected slowly. A lateral film is taken immediately (using a horizontal ray) and examined before proceeding further. (This is to ensure that air is entering the ventricles. If not, careful adjustment of the degree of flexion of the head will have to be made. This film also demonstrates the aqueduct and 4th ventricle in the posterior fossa. Further detail of these structures may be shown by AUTO-TOMOGRAPHY, q.v.)

   A further 5–7 ml of gas are then injected, and PA and lateral views taken. In all, up to 40 ml of gas are introduced, 5 ml at a time, allowing an equal amount of CSF to escape in between. To fill the basal cisterns, an extra 5–10 ml of gas are introduced with the neck extended. Films are taken in various positions which between them will provide a complete outline of the ventricular and cisternal systems.

   A typical sequence would be:

   a. Patient erect—lateral with horizontal beam.

   b. Patient erect—postero-anterior with radiographic base-line horizontal and the central ray 25° towards the head (reverse Townes).

   c. Patient supine—lateral with horizontal beam ('shoot-through').

   d. Patient supine—anteroposterior with chin slightly raised until the radiographic base-line is tilted up 5° from the vertical. Centre between the orbits with the central ray at right-angles to the film.

   e. Patient supine—with the radiographic base-line at

right-angles to the film, centre 2 in (5 cm) above the bridge of the nose, the central ray directed 25° to the feet.

  f. Patient prone—lateral with horizontal beam ('shoot-through').

  g. Patient prone—head in postero-anterior position with the radiographic base-line at right-angles to the film. Centre 1 in (2·5 cm) above the bridge of the nose with the central ray at right-angles to the film.

  h. Patient prone—lateral films with the head turned to each side in turn.

  Note: This positioning depends on the principle that gas floats on top of liquid; thus, when the patient is 'face-up' the anterior parts of the ventricles will be outlined, and when 'face-down' the posterior parts.

  2. The Cisternal Method is similar to the above, except that the gas is introduced directly into the cisterna magna by means of a needle inserted below the occipital region.

ENDOSCOPIC RETROGRADE CHOLANGIOGRAPHY AND PANCREATOGRAPHY (ERCP). The pancreas is one of the most difficult organs to visualize radiographically. Ultrasound is now probably the most effective examination, together with computerized tomography, where available.

  ERCP is a method whereby the pancreatic duct is directly catheterized from the descending duodenum via a flexible fibreoptic endoscope under general anaesthesia, and contrast medium is injected with screen control. This method can also be used for retrograde visualization of the biliary ducts.

ENLARGEMENT TECHNIQUES. Macroradiography (q.v.) has certain limitations. It will always produce blurring at least the size of the focal spot when using ×2 magnification. Also, since the rating of a 0·3 mm focus is limited, exposures may be fairly long which will give rise to the possibility of patient movement, which is also magnified. This, coupled with the fact that a 0·3 mm focus is not available in every department, limits the use of this technique. An alternative is to use photographic, or even direct, optical enlargement. If the object can be placed very close to the film, e.g. scaphoid, an exposure can be made using the normal fine focus on to a very fine grain film. This can then be viewed with a magnifying glass, or photographically enlarged up to 4 or 5 times before the geometric unsharpness becomes noticeable. Suitable film would be one of the single emulsion mammography films available in its special cassette.

  If the object cannot be placed closer than 10 cm from the film (using 90 cm FFD), then macroradiography may produce better results.

ETHMOID SINUSES.   *See* SINUSES.

EXCRETION UROGRAPHY.   *See* INTRAVENOUS UROGRAPHY.

EYE.   To demonstrate the presence of radiopaque foreign bodies in the orbital cavity.

TECHNIQUE.   With the head in the true lateral position, one exposure is made with the eyes looking straight ahead. A non-screen film is used to avoid the possibility of any mark or blemish on the screens being mistaken for the FB. If this film shows an apparent FB the following views should be taken for confirmation:

1. **Lateral.**   With the head in the true lateral position, two exposures are made on one film, the first with the eyes raised, the second with them lowered. If the FB changes in position with the movement of the eye, then it must be in the eyeball or in its muscles.

2. **Occipitomental.**   This should also be taken on a non-screen film. If a localizing cone is used, adequate contrast can be obtained without the use of a Potter-Bucky, which would necessitate an excessively long exposure.

   With the patient prone or erect, nose and chin on the film, adjust the head so that the radiographic base-line is at 45° to the film and the median-sagittal plane perpendicular to the film. Centre to the midline, between the orbits.

   Note: It may sometimes be possible to demonstrate an FB on the lateral view which is too small to be seen on the occipitomental; but any FB which is demonstrated on the occipitomental film must also be demonstrable on the lateral. (For details of accurate localization methods, reference should be made to larger textbooks.)

FACIAL BONES

1. **Occipitomental.**   Patient prone or seated, nose and chin resting on the table with the radiographic base-line 45° to the film and the median-sagittal plane perpendicular to the film. Centre between the lower border of the orbits, with the central ray perpendicular to the film.

   Note: In badly injured patients it may be necessary to reverse this position, i.e. with patient supine and film under head, the central ray is adjusted so that it is angled upwards at 45° to the radiographic base-line. If the patient's chin is raised considerably, this will make the central ray almost vertical and minimize distortion. Centre midway between the lower borders of the orbits.

2. **30° Occipitomental.** With the patient in the same position as above, centre to the lower orbital margin with the central ray tilted 30° to the feet. (This view often demonstrates the lower border of the orbit and the zygoma better than the straight occipitomental.)

3. **Lateral.** With the head in the true lateral position against the film, centre 2·5 cm (1 in) below the outer canthus of the eye. (A non-screen film placed on top of the cassette and exposed simultaneously will give a good view of the nasal bones and the anterior nasal spine of the maxillae.)

See also MAXILLA and ZYGOMA.

FEMORAL ARTERIOGRAPHY. To demonstrate the femoral artery and its branches. Various methods are in use, the commonest being as follows:

1. **Retrograde.** A short catheter is introduced retrogradely via the opposite femoral artery (as in AORTOGRAPHY, q.v.) until its tip lies above the aortic bifurcation. Contrast medium is then introduced and films taken in sequence down the leg using a programmed moving top table and serial changer.

2. **Translumbar.** When the retrograde approach cannot be used because of advanced arteriosclerosis, a translumbar approach may be made as in direct aortography (q.v.). Using a sliding table-top, films are taken as above.

3. **Direct.** This is not used frequently nowadays but is sometimes the method of choice, for instance in cases of trauma where there is a possibility of rupture of the femoral artery associated with a fracture of the femoral shaft.

A needle is inserted directly into the artery in the groin just below the inguinal ligament and contrast medium injected rapidly. Radiographs are taken as in 1 and 2 above, or serially of the localized area under investigation.

FEMUR

1. **Anteroposterior.** Patient supine with the leg extended and the foot of the affected side vertical. The film must include at least one joint, and should therefore be displaced towards the end of the bone most suspect. If a view of the complete shaft is essential, then a separate film must be taken of the other end. Centre to the middle of the film.

2. **Lateral.** Patient supine, half turned to the affected side, the leg being rotated outwards until the knee is in the true lateral position. The same remarks apply as for the AP film.

Lateral (alternative view when it is not possible to turn the patient). Patient supine as for the AP view. If the lower half is suspect, place the film vertically between the legs and direct the horizontal beam from the affected side; or if the upper half is under examination, place the film vertically against the outer side of the affected leg and raise the sound leg out of the path of the horizontal beam, resting it (with the knee bent) on a stool or pillows. In this latter view it may be desirable to angle the central beam 25–30° towards the head to avoid superimposing the thigh muscles of the unaffected leg on to the head and neck of the femur of the affected leg.

See also HIP JOINT and KNEE JOINT.

FETUS. *See* PREGNANCY.

FIBULA
  1. **Anteroposterior.** Patient supine, with the leg slightly rotated inwards, to project both upper and lower ends of the fibula away from the tibia. The film should include both joints, but if this is not possible the joint at the end under suspicion should be included. Centre to the middle of the film.
  2. **Lateral.** Patient supine, half rotated to the affected side, with the leg rotated to the true lateral position. Centre to the middle of the film.
     Lateral (alternative view when it is not possible to turn the patient). Place soft pads under the affected limb to raise it 5·0–7·5 cm (2–3 in) above the table. Place the film vertically between the legs and direct the central beam horizontally from the affected side to the middle of the film.

See also ANKLE JOINT, KNEE JOINT and TIBIA.

FINGERS. *See* HAND.

FOOT. Four views are in general use. For bony injuries the first three should be used; for bony pathology the first and second; and for localization of foreign bodies the first and last.
  1. **Anteroposterior (or Dorsiplantar).** Patient sitting on the table with the foot resting flat on the film and the two knees against one another to provide support. Centre to the cuboid/navicular region.
  2. **Anteroposterior Oblique (or Dorsiplantar oblique).** Patient seated on the table with the foot resting on the film as for the previous position. Then rotate the knee of the affected side inwards so that the foot is turned on to its inner aspect until

the dorsum is horizontal with the table top. Centre to the cuboid/navicular region with 15° tilt towards the ankle.

3. **Lateral Oblique.** Position as for lateral view. The patient is further rotated until the knee rests on the table. In this position the foot is allowed to roll obliquely forward. Centre to the base of the fifth metatarsal.

4. **Lateral.** With the patient half lying on the affected side and the limb rotated outwards, the foot is adjusted until the plantar surface is at right-angles to the film. Centre to the middle of the foot (i.e., about the cuneiform region).

See also CALCANEUM and SUBTALOID JOINT.

FORAMEN MAGNUM. To show bony pathology or fractures of the skull extending into the foramen magnum.

TECHNIQUE. Two views may be useful to demonstrate this region, 35° fronto-occipital and submentovertical. For positioning, *see* SKULL.

FOREARM

1. **Anteroposterior.** Patient seated with the forearm resting on the film, and the elbow in the true AP position, the back of the hand flat on the table. Centre to the middle of the film, to include both the elbow and wrist joints.

2. **Lateral.** Elbow and wrist in the true lateral position with the upper and lower arm resting on the table. Centre to the middle of the film.

See also ELBOW JOINT and WRIST JOINT.

FOREIGN BODY. A foreign body can be demonstrated only if it possesses a greater degree of radiopacity than its surroundings, or if it can be coated with a radiopaque substance.

In Eye. *See* EYE.

Ingested. The majority of FBs swallowed will pass readily into the stomach and through the small and large intestines without hold-up. Small fish or meat bones may 'catch' in the wall of the pharynx or upper oesophagus. In this case the patient may feel that 'something has stuck in his throat' and can give an indication of its position. The only view to demonstrate this adequately is a lateral film of the soft tissues of the neck. (Position as for lateral cervical vertebrae.)

A non-opaque fishbone may be demonstrated by coating it with barium during a barium swallow, but *on no account* should this be done without the consent of the ENT surgeon who may be called upon to remove it.

Large safety-pins or hair-grips may obstruct in the pyloric end of the stomach, and straight AP films of good quality covering the whole gastrointestinal tract are usually sufficient; but lateral views should also be taken if suspected FBs are not located on these.

Inhaled. If there is any possibility of the FB having been inhaled into the lungs, chest films will also have to be taken. Large FBs may cause a segment of lung to collapse and this can be demonstrated, although the FB itself may be non-opaque.

Soft Tissues. When small FBs of dubious opacity are sought in the soft tissues (e.g., glass, plastic or wood splinters in the hand) best quality films are required, preferably non-screen, to avoid confusion with screen blemishes. For precise methods of localization, reference should be made to larger text-books. Generally speaking, AP and lateral views should be taken of the area concerned, but in certain cases, e.g. scalp, tangential views may be helpful.

FRONTAL BONE. *See* SKULL.

FRONTAL SINUSES. *See* SINUSES.

GALLBLADDER (Straight). To demonstrate opaque stone formation in the gallbladder or biliary ducts.

Postero-anterior. Patient prone with the left arm by the side and the right hand resting on the pillow beside the head. This will rotate the right side of the body slightly away from the film. Centre 10 cm (4 in) to the right of the spine, at the level of the lower costal margin.

Note: In many departments ultrasound examination is now the initial method of choice.

See also CHOLECYSTANGIOGRAPHY, CHOLECYSTOGRAPHY and ULTRASOUND.

GASTROINTESTINAL TRACT. *See* ABDOMEN and BARIUM EXAMINATIONS.

GRAHAM'S TEST. *See* CHOLECYSTOGRAPHY (ORAL).

HAMATE. *See* WRIST JOINT.

HAND
1. **Postero-anterior.** The hand is placed palm downwards on the film, fingers slightly separated. Centre to the head of the metacarpal of the middle finger.

2. **Oblique.** From the PA position the hand is rotated 45° towards the true lateral. Centre to the head of the metacarpal of the little finger.

3. **Lateral.** The hand is placed in the true lateral position, with fingers outstretched and thumb resting forward on a non-opaque pad. Centre to the head of the metacarpal of the index finger. *Note:* In this view the carpal bones are super-imposed. This view is essential, however, when it is necessary to localize a foreign body in the hand.

Lateral View of Fingers. For the index and middle fingers the hand is rotated inwards from the PA position until the index finger is resting on the film; the middle finger is supported on a non-opaque pad and the other two fingers flexed to the palm.

For the ring and little fingers, the hand is placed in the true lateral position with the little finger partially flexed and resting on the film; the ring finger is supported on a non-opaque pad and the other two fingers flexed to the palm. If all the fingers are required, position as for a lateral hand, but separate the fingers supporting the ring, middle and index fingers on non-opaque pads.

HEART. *See* ANGIOCARDIOGRAPHY, AORTA, BARIUM SWALLOW, CHEST, CORONARY ARTERIOGRAPHY and MEDIASTINUM.

HEPATO-LIENOGRAPHY. *See* PORTAL VENOGRAPHY.

HIP JOINT

1. **Anteroposterior (One hip).** Patient supine with the feet rotated slightly inwards. The heels should be approximately 5 cm (2 in) apart and the big toes touching, the feet being immobilized in this position with sand-bags. Centre to a point 2·5 cm (1 in) perpendicularly below the midpoint of a line joining the anterior superior iliac spine and the symphysis pubis.

2. **Lateral (One hip).** Rotate the patient half-way on to the affected side, and rotate the leg until the knee rests on the table. Centre to the femoral pulse in the crease of the groin.

3. **Lateral Neck of Femur.** Patient supine with the affected leg straight and the foot vertical. The film and grid are positioned vertically and pressed into the side of the patient just above the iliac crest, the film approximately parallel to the neck of the femur. Centre to the neck of femur, using a horizontal ray at right-angles to the film. The sound leg is lifted out of the way of the beam and rested on a stool on the table.

4. **Anteroposterior (Both hips).** Patient supine with feet as in the AP view above. Centre 2·5 cm (1 in) above the symphysis pubis.

5. **Lateral (Both hips).** From the AP position draw the patient's knees up until the feet are flat on the table, then rotate the legs outwards as far as possible (45–60°) resting the soles of the feet together. Make sure that the pelvis is not disturbed from the true AP position during the movement. Centre 2·5 cm (1 in) above the symphysis pubis.

HUMERUS

1. **Anteroposterior.** The film should include both the shoulder and elbow joints. The patient is placed supine or erect, and rotated a little to the affected side so that the humerus can rest on the film, with the elbow adjusted so that it is in the true AP position. Centre to the middle of the film.

2. **Lateral.** This is easier to take erect, as the patient should be facing the film. Bend the elbow and take the forearm across the abdomen, supporting it with the other hand. Rest the humerus against the film and centre to the middle of the film.

See also ELBOW JOINT and SHOULDER JOINT.

HYSTEROSALPINGOGRAPHY.

HYSTEROSALPINGOGRAPHY. To demonstrate the uterus and Fallopian tubes, in particular the patency of the latter, by means of a contrast medium. This examination is most frequently employed in the investigation of infertility.

TECHNIQUE. The contrast medium is introduced directly into the cervix of the uterus by the gynaecologist under the screen control of the radiologist, who takes films at his discretion.

ILEUM. *See* BARIUM EXAMINATIONS.

ILIUM

1. **Anteroposterior.** Patient supine with the posterior superior iliac spine in the midline of the table, and about 2 in (5 cm) below the upper margin of the film. Centre to the middle of the film.

2. **Oblique.** From the AP position rotate the patient 45° to the affected side, making sure that the ilium is not displaced off the film. Centre to the middle of the film.

Note: It is preferable to take an AP film of the whole pelvis, rather than of one side. It is unwise to attempt the oblique view in cases of gross injury to the pelvis.

INTERCONDYLAR NOTCH (of femur). *See* KNEE JOINT.

INTERNAL AUDITORY MEATUS. Three views will generally suffice:
1. 35° Fronto-occipital.
2. Submentovertical.
3. Anteroposterior (perorbital).

For positioning, *see* PETROUS TEMPORAL BONE.

These views may be replaced or supplemented by tomography in the AP (perorbital) position. In view of the possibility of radiation damage to the cornea of the eye, lead eyeshields are recommended. If the tomography is performed using circular or hypocycloidal blurring, the shields will not be projected over the area under examination.

COMPUTERIZED TOMOGRAPHY, where available, is the method of choice.

INTERVENTIONAL RADIOLOGY. This is a relatively new term used to cover those methods which are now entering the field of diagnostic radiologists which are, strictly speaking, for treatment rather than simply for diagnosis. At present these comprise principally angioplasty and embolization, but also include nephrostomy, abscess drainage, gallstone removal and biliary drainage.

Percutaneous Transluminal Angioplasty (PTA). This is a technique whereby vascular stenoses may be dilated by means of a balloon catheter intoduced on a guide-wire (usually through the femoral artery) under X-ray control into various arteries e.g. iliac, femoral, popliteal or renal, and then inflated to break down the atheroma and open up the lumen. Another use for this method is in some patients shown on arteriography to have coronary artery stenosis. Only about 10 per cent of those shown to have stenoses are suitable for PTA, but in these a high proportion can be successfully dilated, although the method is not without its dangers and there is a high re-stenosis rate. An even newer, and still experimental, method of clearing a blocked artery is by the use of a laser beam probe.

Transluminal Embolization. Bleeding from, for instance, peptic ulcers or other parts of the GI tract may be controlled in some cases by the blocking off of the appropriate artery by the direct insertion of a chemical or gel foam through the catheter. This method can also be used for the treatment of vascular malformations in various parts of the body into which small mechanical emboli are introduced e.g. in the shape of a tiny 'umbrella' or coiled spring.

INTESTINE (Large and small). *See* ABDOMEN and BARIUM EXAMINATIONS.

INTRAVENOUS UROGRAPHY (IVU). To demonstrate the kidneys, ureters, and bladder (also known as INTRAVENOUS PYELOGRAPHY (IVP).

TECHNIQUE. Fluid intake is normally forbidden for 6 hr prior to the examination and the patient is encouraged to be as ambulant as possible to keep bowel gas to a minimum.

Control films of the renal tract are taken to ascertain that the renal areas are free from bowel gas; 25–100 ml of the contrast medium are then injected intravenously, depending on the type of contrast medium used and the size of the patient. A compression band is applied to the lower abdomen to compress the ureters and delay the passage of the medium down the ureters from the renal pelves. Films are taken at intervals, the precise timing being at the discretion of the individual radiologist. A typical sequence would be:

> 5 min after injection (in expiration);
> 10 min after injection (in inspiration);
> 20 min after injection (in expiration).

If the pelvicaliceal pattern on either side is obscured by bowel contents, a narrow-angle tomographic cut (at about 7–9 cm depending on the size of the patient) may give more satisfactory visualization.

The compression is then released and a film may be taken of the whole urinary tract in an attempt to demonstrate the ureters and bladder. Alternatively, a film of the bladder only may be taken, followed by a further film after micturition, when required.

In cases of suspected ureteric obstruction, where no function is shown in one kidney up to 30 min, further films may be taken up to 24 hr, when delayed filling may be observed.

Note: It is imperative to ask the patient prior to this examination whether there is any known sensitivity to iodine compounds or any other 'allergic' history. The possibility of any reaction to the contrast medium is negligible with the use of low-osmolar products.

See also RADIO-ISOTOPE IMAGING, RETROGRADE PYELOGRAPHY and URINARY TRACT.

ISCHIUM

Anteroposterior. Patient supine with the symphysis pubis to the midline of the table. Centre to the symphysis pubis. A film taken in the same way, but with a 20° tilt to the head, may also be useful.

ISOTOPE SCANNING. *See* RADIO-ISOTOPE IMAGING.

JEJUNUM. *See* BARIUM EXAMINATIONS.

JUGULAR FORAMEN. To demonstrate the comparative size of the foramina.

TECHNIQUE

1. **Submentovertical.** Patient erect or supine. The neck is hyperextended so that the vertex rests on the film. Support should be given to the shoulders before tilting the head back. The median-sagittal plane is perpendicular. Centre between the external auditory meati with the tube angled so that the central ray makes an angle of 70° to the radiographic base-line.

2. **Lateral.** Head in true lateral position, then rotate it 15° towards the film. Centre just below the external auditory meatus in contact with the table with a tilt of 15° towards the feet. Take both sides for comparison.

KIDNEYS. *See* INTRAVENOUS UROGRAPHY, RADIO-ISOTOPE IMAGING, RENAL ARTERIOGRAPHY, RENAL CALCULI, RENAL PUNCTURE, RETROGRADE PYELOGRAPHY, ULTRASOUND IMAGING and URINARY TRACT.

KNEE JOINT

1. **Anteroposterior.** Patient sitting or lying on the table with the leg flat, and the knee in contact with the film. With the foot upright, rotate the leg inwards so that the patella is centralized over the femur. Centre to the knee joint 1·25 cm (½ in) below the patella.

2. **Lateral.** Rotate the patient on to the affected side, the ankle being raised on a sand-bag and the knee resting on the film. Centre 2·5 cm (1 in) below and 2·5 cm (1 in) behind the lower border of the patella.

3. **Oblique.** This may be taken in either the PA or AP position, the leg being rotated approximately 45° to either side in turn. Centre to the joint.

4. **Tunnel Views.** These views demonstrate the intercondylar notch and may help to confirm the presence of loose bodies in the joint. The position is the same for both views, the only difference being the tube angulation. *Either* the patient should be in the AP position with the knee flexed and resting on a curved cassette which is supported on a sand-bag. *Or* if a

curved cassette is not available, then the patient can kneel on the affected side with the film placed under the knee. A sand-bag should be placed under the ankle to take the weight of the leg off the toes. The patient then leans forward so that the femur is approximately 45° to the table. Centre for both positions to the knee joint. For the AP view, one film is taken with the central ray at right-angles to the lower leg, and the other with the central ray at 110° to the lower leg. For the PA views the angles are 90° and 70° respectively.

See also ARTHROGRAPHY and PATELLA.

LACRIMAL DUCTS. *See* DACRYOCYSTOGRAPHY.

LARYNX. Tomography is the method of choice and films should be taken in the AP position. When the correct level has been established, a further cut should be made with the patient phonating 'E' during the exposure.

Laryngography is sometimes valuable whereby a contrast medium is slowly introduced over the back of the tongue while the patient breathes.

LOWER JAW. *See* MANDIBLE.

LUMBAR RADICULOGRAPHY. *See* MYELOGRAPHY.

LUMBAR VERTEBRAE
1. **Anteroposterior.** Patient supine. Centre to the midline at the level of the lower costal margin. (It is advisable to raise the patient's knees off the table, placing sand-bags on the feet to help maintain this position, as this will help to reduce the lumbar curvature. The shoulders should also be raised on pillows.)
2. **Lateral.** Patient lying in the lateral position with his hands on the pillow by his head, and knees flexed to give stability. Centre to the level of the lower costal margin, 7·5–10 cm (3–4 in) anterior to the third lumbar spinous process. (Under routine conditions it is usually advisable to take an extra lateral view of the L.5/S.1 area, as the pelvis tends to obscure this region on the above film, unless a high kV technique is employed. *See* LUMBOSACRAL ARTICULATION.)
3. **Oblique.** From the AP position, rotate the patient above 45° to each side in turn. Centre to the spine, at the level of the lower costal margin.
Note: This view is of particular value in cases of suspected spondylolisthesis. The side demonstrated is the side nearest to the film.

LUMBOSACRAL ARTICULATION.

1. **Anteroposterior.** Patient supine, as for AP lumbar spine. Centre to the midline at the level of the anterior superior iliac spines, the central ray being directed 10–25° towards the head, according to the type of patient and the curvature of the spine. (Men usually require about 10° and women 20–25°.) Even further tilting may be necessary in some cases and it should be borne in mind that the film itself will have to be moved upwards, otherwise the joint will be projected off the film.

2. **Lateral.** Patient lying in the true lateral position as for lumbar spine. Centre 7·5 cm (3 in) anterior to the spinous process of L.5. (The level is 2·5 cm (1 in) below the anterior superior iliac spine.) A localizing cone should always be used. *Note:* Minor degrees of spondylolisthesis may only be demonstrated on an erect film.

3. **Oblique.** Patient in the same position as for oblique lumbar spine. Centre 5 cm (2 in) medial to the anterior superior iliac spine, with the central ray directed 10° to the head.

LUNATE. *See* WRIST JOINT.

LYMPHOGRAPHY. To demonstrate the lymphatic channels and lymph glands. In many cases CT scanning has replaced this examination in the visualization of enlarged glands.

TECHNIQUE

1. **Lower Limb.** With the patient supine on the X-ray table 2 ml of an aqueous solution of patent blue dye (10 per cent) are injected into the web spaces of the toes. This is taken up by the lymphatics which appear as blue streaks under the skin. An incision is then made on the dorsum of the foot under local anaesthesia to expose a lymphatic vessel; and, using a fine needle with tubing attached, up to 10 ml of an oil contrast medium are injected very slowly. Films are taken as required over several hours.

2. **Pelvis and Abdomen.** Either the above technique may be used, with films taken from about 20 min up to 24 hr; or a similar procedure may be carried out, injecting the blue dye into the foot, followed 10–15 min later by instillation of the contrast medium into an exposed lymphatic vessel in the groin. Films are taken up to 24 hr.

3. **Arm.** The procedure is as above, the incision being made in the axilla after injection of the dye into the finger webs.

MACRORADIOGRAPHY. Macroradiography is the technique of producing radiographs where the enlargement distortion is

considerably higher than normal, and is usually of the order of twice the original size. To achieve this and at the same time retain good definition, a very fine focus tube is needed with a focal spot size of 0·3 mm square. To obtain a ×2 enlargement the film must be supported as far below the subject as the focal spot is above it.

The technique is not widely used at present, but it may be of help in the diagnosis of fractures of the wrist joint, and also may prove of value in showing some of the finer structures in the skull. Positioning is very critical and great care is needed in centering. Because of the distance between the subject and the film, a large proportion of the secondary radiation will not reach the film and in all cases satisfactory films may be obtained without the use of Potter-Bucky or grid mechanisms. An increase of about 20 kV will, however, be required to compensate for this loss in secondary radiation.

See also ENLARGEMENT TECHNIQUES.

MAGNETIC RESONANCE IMAGING (MRI), also known as Nuclear Magnetic Resonance (NMR). The introduction of this newest technology rivals the CT scanner in demonstrating the brain and spinal cord and is superior in showing lesions of the posterior fossa and brain stem. It is very useful in cases of spinal trauma and disc prolapse, as well as to display the orbits and sinuses.

Thoracic and abdominal organs can also be imaged, for instance, the cortex and medulla of the kidneys can be differentiated, thus providing the promise of accurate diagnosis in renal failure. It is also possible to differentiate between the grey and white matter of the brain and to demonstrate the lesions of multiple sclerosis. It may prove possible to distinguish between benign and malignant tumours.

MRI does not use ionizing radiation, is non-invasive and, like CT imaging, does not rely on the use of catheters or contrast media, although special ones are now coming into use to enhance the images.

The principle of an MR imager is that the presence of a magnetic field can influence the resonance (behaviour) of protons in the nuclei of atoms, usually the hydrogen atom. By varying the strength of the magnetic field, changes in cell biochemistry can be demonstrated and hence changes in the composition of tissues, so that abnormalities of cell structure can be detected.

The heart of the system is a large cylindrical magnet, in the centre of which the patient is placed. Radio waves are pulsed into the patient and these, together with the magnetic field, cause the protons in the atomic nuclei to tilt like tiny bar magnets. When the proton returns to its former position, it emits further radio waves which enable its position to be determined. This allows us to plot the distribution of hydrogen atoms in the organ under investigation, and with the use of computers, 'slice' or 3D pictures can be produced.

There are still few of these machines in operation in the UK, and they are more expensive than a CT imager. It seems likely that they will be found only in specialized units in the foreseeable future (mainly neuroradiological), although mobile MR (and CT) imagers are now obtainable so that a group of hospitals can share one machine.

MALAR BONES.   *See* FACIAL BONES, MAXILLA and ZYGOMA.

MAMMOGRAPHY.   To demonstrate tissue changes in the breast.

For the highest quality films a kilovoltage of 25–30 is recommended, but adequate radiographs can be obtained with 40 kV (the minimum of most generators in standard use), provided care is given to the choice of films. Aluminium filters should be removed from the tube if possible.

There are at present several film or film-screen combinations which give excellent results, including Xerography (q.v.).

POSITIONING.   Because of the variability in size, shape and mobility of the breast, it is impossible to lay down precise positioning techniques. Exposures may be made with the patient seated, supine or standing. The most suitable will have to be determined at the time of examination.

1. **Supero-inferior (Cranio-caudal).**   The film holder is placed under the breast and pressed against the chest wall. Centre to the base of the breast using a localizing cone. The nipple should be in profile.

2. **Lateral (Medial or Latero-medial).**   Patient rotated to the affected side, approximately 45° with the breast resting against the film. Centre to the base of the breast with the nipple in profile.

3. **Oblique.**   This view is an attempt to include the maximum amount of breast tissue on the one film and positioning is essentially a matter of judgement.

4. **Axilla.**   Patient rotated approximately 30° to the affected side. The humerus should be at right-angles to the body. Centre 5 cm (2 in) below the axilla.

MANDIBLE
1. **Postero-anterior.** Patient prone or erect with the head positioned as for the PA skull view. Centre 6·25 cm (2½ in) below the radiographic base-line, the central ray at right-angles to the film.
2. **Lateral.** Patient erect or prone with the head in the true lateral position. Centre midway between the external auditory meatus and symphysis menti.
3. **Oblique.** With the head in the true lateral position, the film is positioned against the affected side. Centre 5 cm (2 in) below the angle of the jaw with the tube tilted 25° to the head: *or* flex the head laterally to the affected side and centre 5 cm (2 in) below the angle of the jaw, keeping the beam horizontal.
4. **Inferosuperior A.** This view is taken when a general view of the mandible is required, to show the amount of displacement in cases of gross injury. Patient supine or erect, with the head in the routine submentovertical position, i.e. with the radiographic base-line as nearly parallel to the film as possible. Centre to the midline, between the angles of the jaw.
5. **Inferosuperior B.** Where the symphysis menti area is required and if the patient's condition permits, an occlusal view of the anterior mandible may be taken. Patient supine or erect. An occlusal film is placed in the mouth as far back as possible and the mouth gently closed on the film to hold it in place. The chin is raised and the tube centred at right-angles to the film.

See also ORTHOPANTOMOGRAPHY, PANAGRAPHY, SYMPHYSIS MENTI and TEMPOROMANDIBULAR JOINTS.

MANUBRIUM STERNI. *See* STERNUM.

MASTOIDS. To demonstrate the air cells.
1. **35° Fronto-occipital.** Patient supine or erect in the true AP position with the median-sagittal plane and radiographic base-line perpendicular to the film. Centre to the midline at the level of the mastoid processes, the central ray being directed 35° to the feet.
2. **Lateral Oblique.** Head in the true lateral position with the median-sagittal plane parallel to the film, and the interorbital line perpendicular to the film. Fold the pinna of the ear in contact with the table forwards, and let the pressure of the head keep it in this position. Centre 1·25 cm (½ in) behind the external auditory meatus in contact with the table, with

the central ray angled 25° to the feet. Always take both sides for comparison.

These two views should be adquate for diagnosis, but some radiologists may require the following view also:

3. **Profile.** Patient supine or erect facing the tube. Rotate the head until the median-sagittal plane is 35° to the perpendicular, and the radiographic base-line is perpendicular to the film. Centre to the mastoid process away from the film, the central ray being angled 25° to the feet. Take both sides for comparison. A small localizing cone is essential.

See also PETROUS TEMPORAL BONE.

MAXILLA

1. **Lateral.** Head in the true lateral position with the median-sagittal plane parallel to the film and the interorbital line perpendicular to the film. Centre 2·5 cm (1 in) below the outer canthus of the eye.

2. **Occlusal or Intra-oral.** A. Patient seated. An occlusal film is placed in the mouth and gently held with the teeth. Centre through the nose with the tube angled at 75° to the film. B. Patient seated. An occlusal film is placed in the mouth but displaced as far as possible to the side under examination. Centre over the roots of the upper premolars, with the tube angled 60° to the film.

3. **Oblique.** Patient prone or erect with the head rotated 45°, and the radiographic base-line tilted upwards 10–15°. Centre through the maxilla with the tube tilted 10° to the head. Both sides should be taken for comparison.

See also FACIAL BONES, ORTHOPANTOMOGRAPHY, PANAGRAPHY and ZYGOMA.

MAXILLARY ANTRA. *See* SINUSES.

MEASUREMENT OF LENGTHS. Accurate measurement of length of limbs may be required for orthopaedic work, and this cannot be assessed from ordinary films because of the enlargement produced. Two simple methods are available.

1. A cassette long enough to cover the entire limb is placed under it and the limb is scanned, using a slit diaphragm. Since the narrow X-ray beam used is always vertical, it follows that the joints on the film must be the same distance apart as they are in the limb itself, no lengthwise distortion having taken place.

2. The same cassette is used and separate exposures are made, carefully centred over each joint in turn. If these are coned

there will be parts of the limb not included on the film, but nevertheless the distance between joint surfaces will be accurate. If a long cassette is not available, separate films may be taken of each joint, carefully centred, with a lead marker on each film at the level of the joint. If the distance between the lead markers is noted, it will be possible to place the films in their identical positions after processing, and so enable accurate measurement to be made.

3. It is possible to obtain a perspex metre rule with radiopaque gradations, and this can be placed beside the leg on either a long cassette or separate cassettes (as in 1 and 2 above) to give direct measurement.

MEDIASTINUM

1. **Postero-anterior.** As for PA chest, with an increase of about 5 kV, to penetrate partially the heart shadow.
2. **Oblique.** The correct positioning for the oblique views should be determined by screening, but if this is not possible the following guide may be helpful:

    Left Anterior Oblique. From the PA position the patient is rotated approximately 70° with the right side away from the film. It may be found easier for the patient to rest his right hand on his head.

    Right Anterior Oblique. From the PA position rotate the patient approximately 60° with the left side away from the film.

    Note the large angles of rotation required for these views. This is necessary to give adequate separation between the heart and the vertebrae.

3. **Lateral.** As for lateral chest. Usually a left lateral view is taken.

    N.B. Tomography may provide further information. Where available, computerized tomography is the method of choice.

METACARPALS. *See* HAND.

METATARSALS. *See* FOOT.

MIDDLE EAR. *See* PETROUS TEMPORAL BONE.

MYELOGRAPHY. To demonstrate lesions of the spinal canal and cord.

  TECHNIQUE. This examination is usually carried out under local anaesthesia, but a general anaesthetic may be used for young children.

The patient is placed in position for a lumbar puncture on the X-ray table, either erect or reclining. The operator inserts a lumbar puncture needle into the spinal canal between the third and fourth lumbar vertebrae and 3–6 ml of the contrast medium are injected. The patient is then placed prone with shoulder supports. By manoeuvring him on the tilting table under screen control, the medium can be made to flow up and down the subarachnoid space surrounding the spinal cord as far as the upper cervical region, and thus any lesion may be outlined or the site of an obstruction accurately delineated. 'Spot' radiographs are taken by the radiologist. In some cases the patient is also screened in the supine position.

If lumbar puncture is not possible or it is desired to define the upper border of a lesion which is causing a complete obstruction, the contrast medium may be introduced below the occiput directly into the cisterna magna (cisternal puncture).

Note: Water-soluble non-ionic contrast media are now used exclusively in this examination as they are: (1) rapidly absorbed from the spinal canal; (2) considerably less toxic and only rarely produce side-effects; and (3) give bettter definition of the nerve roots. This property is particularly useful in the lumbar region when looking for prolapsed discs (LUMBAR RADICULOGRAPHY).

NASAL BONES. To demonstrate fractures and degree of displacement of the nasal bones and septum.

TECHNIQUE

1. **Lateral.** Patient supine or erect with the head in the true lateral position. Centre to the root of the nose.
2. **Supero-inferior.** This is a useful additional view, although it is not possible in every subject, as the frontal bone or upper jaw may obscure the nasal bones. Patient erect or supine. Place an occlusal film just inside the mouth and instruct the patient to hold it gently with his teeth, so that approximately two-thirds of the film project. Centre from above, care being taken to get as much of the nasal bones free from obstruction as possible.

Note: An occipitomental view is also useful in determining whether or not deviation of the nasal septum has taken place. For positioning, *see* FACIAL BONES.

NASOPHARYNX. *See* ADENOIDS.

NAVICULAR. *See* FOOT.

NECK OF FEMUR. *See* HIP JOINT.

NUCLEAR MAGNETIC RESONANCE (NMR). *See* MAGNETIC RESONANCE IMAGING.

OCCIPITAL BONE. *See* SKULL.

ODONTOID PROCESS
1. **Anteroposterior.** Patient erect or supine with the head in the true AP position and the radiographic base-line tilted upwards 12°. Centre through the open mouth, the central ray at right angles to film. *Note:* This view is easiest in the edentulous subject, and dentures must always be removed. Also make sure that the base-line angle is not increased when the patient opens his mouth.
2. **Lateral.** Positioning as for lateral cervical vertebrae, but centre to C.2, i.e., 2·5 cm (1 in) below the external auditory meatus. Take flexion and extension views in cases of suspected subluxation, provided that a fracture has been excluded.

Note: If a fracture is suspected, the examination should be carried out in the supine position and with the minimum possible movement of the patient, using a horizontal beam for the lateral view.

OESOPHAGUS. *See* BARIUM SWALLOW and FOREIGN BODY.

OLECRANON PROCESS. *See* ELBOW JOINT.

OPTIC FORAMEN. To demonstrate variations in the size of the optic foramina.
TECHNIQUE
Oblique. Place the orbit of the side under examination directly over the film, resting the forehead, cheek, and nose on the table. Adjust the head so that the median-sagittal plane and the radiographic base-line are both 35° from the perpendicular. Centre through the orbit in contact with the table. Both sides are taken for comparison.

ORBIT. *See* FACIAL BONES and MAXILLA.

ORBITAL VENOGRAPHY. This may be carried out by direct puncture of the frontal vein in the investigation of proptosis, orbital masses, and cavernous sinus thrombosis. *See also* COMPUTERIZED TOMOGRAPHY and MAGNETIC RESONANCE IMAGING.

ORTHOPANTOMOGRAPHY (OPG).   This technique is used to produce a radiograph of the complete mandible, maxilla, and teeth on a single film using special apparatus in which the X-ray tube and a curved cassette rotate around the patient during the exposure. It can also be used in the examination of temporo-mandibular joints.

PANAGRAPHY.   This technique produces a film of the complete upper or lower dental arches, using special apparatus. The anode of the special X-ray tube is inserted into the mouth, and the film in a flexible cassette is wrapped around the upper or lower jaw as required.

PANCREAS.   See CT IMAGING, ERCP and ULTRASOUND IMAGING.

PARIETAL BONE.   See SKULL.

PAROTID GLAND.   To demonstrate stone formation in the parotid gland and duct.
TECHNIQUE
  1. **Lateral.**   As for MANDIBLE.
  2. **Postero-anterior Profile.**   Positioning as for PA mandible. If a non-screen film is placed on top of a loaded cassette and both films exposed simultaneously, a very small calculus which may otherwise have been overpenetrated may be revealed.
See also SIALOGRAPHY.

PATELLA.   In cases of suspected injury, AP, lateral, and oblique films only should be taken, but if it is desired to see the infrapatellar surface an inferosuperior view must also be taken.
  1. **Anteroposterior.**   Positioning as for AP knee, but increase the exposure to penetrate the femur adequately.
  2. **Lateral.**   As for lateral knee. It may be helpful to take this film with the patient supine, using a horizontal beam centred to the patella. This will avoid unnecessary movement of the knee.
  3. **Oblique.**   Positioning as for AP. The patient is then rotated 45° to alternate sides. *Note:* This view projects alternate halves of the patella free from the underlying femur.
  4. **Inferosuperior.**   This may be taken in two ways, the first only being used when the patient can bend his knee without difficulty:
    A. Patient prone with the knee of the affected side flexed and the leg raised vertically, steadied by a bandage around the

ankle running over the shoulder and held by the patient. Centre to the inferior surface of the patella, the tube tilted 15° to the lower leg.

B. Patient supine with the knee flexed over sand-bags or pillows and the film supported along the femur. Centre to the patella, the tube tilted 15° to the lower leg.

See also KNEE JOINT.

PELVIMETRY. *See* PREGNANCY.

PELVIS

1. **Anteroposterior.** Patient supine, feet together. Centre about 5 cm (2 in) above the symphysis pubis.

2. **Oblique.** This is taken of each side separately, if the condition of the patient permits. From the AP position rotate the patient 30° to the affected side. Centre about 2·5 cm (1 in) about the hip joint.

See also ILIUM, ISCHIUM, and PUBIS.

PETROUS TEMPORAL BONE. The positioning given may be used on a general purpose table as well as on a specialized skull unit. Five views are described and should prove adequate for this region. It must be emphasized that the highest quality films should be obtained (using localizing cones at all times) in view of the small size of the structures under examination.

1. **Lateral.** Patient prone or erect, with the head in the true lateral position, the median-sagittal plane parallel to, and the interorbital line perpendicular to the film. Centre 5 cm (2 in) above the external auditory meatus away from the film with the tube angled 25° to the feet.

2. **35° Fronto-occipital (Anteroposterior half axial).** Patient supine or erect in the true AP position, with the median-sagittal plane and the radiographic base-line perpendicular to the film. Centre 7·5 cm (3 in) above the bridge of the nose, with the tube angled 35° towards the feet.

3. **Submentovertical (Axial).** Patient erect or supine. The neck is hyperextended so that the vertex rests on the film. Support is given to the shoulders before tilting the head back. The median-sagittal plane is perpendicular. The radiographic base-line is parallel to the film. Centre midway between the angles of the jaw, with the central ray at right-angles to the base-line.

4. **Anteroposterior (Perorbital).** Patient supine or erect, with the head in the true AP position. The median-sagittal plane and the radiographic base-line are perpendicular to the film.

Centre in the midline to the interorbital line, with the tub
perpendicular, so that the petrous temporal region is pro
jected through the orbits.

5. **Postero-anterior oblique (Stenver's).** Patient prone o
erect. The orbit of the side being examined is placed over the
film. The radiographic base-line is perpendicular to the film
and the median-sagittal plane is at 45° to the film. Centre
midway between the external auditory meatus and the
external occipital protuberance, with the central ray angled
12° towards the head.

Note: In some cases tomography may be necessary to
supplement these films: for instance, at 2 mm intervals in
the AP position, from the external auditory meatu
backwards.

See also APPENDIX 5.

PHALANGES. *See* FOOT and HAND.

PHARYNX. *See* ADENOIDS and FOREIGN BODY.

PHLEBOGRAPHY. *See* VENOGRAPHY.

PISIFORM. *See* WRIST JOINT.

PITUITARY FOSSA. To demonstrate enlargement or erosion
of the sella turcica or abnormal calcification in this area.

TECHNIQUE

1. **Lateral.** Head in the true lateral position, with the
median-sagittal plane parallel to the film, and the inter
orbital line perpendicular. Centre 2·5 cm (1 in) above and
2·5 cm (1 in) in front of the external auditory meatus. A
small localizing cone is essential.

2. **Fronto-occipital (Anteroposterior half axial).** Patient in
the true AP position with the median-sagittal plane and the
radiographic base-line perpendicular to the film. Centre
7·5 cm (3 in) above the bridge of the nose, with the tube
angled 35° to the feet. A localizing cone is used.

3. **20° Occipitofrontal (Inclined postero-anterior).** Head in
the true PA position, with the median-sagittal plane and
the radiographic base-line perpendicular to the film
Centre in the midline to the interorbital line, with the
central ray angled 20° to the feet.

PORTAL VENOGRAPHY. To outline the portal vein and its
tributaries by the injection of contrast medium. Several
methods are in common use:

1. **Operative.**   When the surgeon has the area exposed at open operation, 20 ml of the contrast medium are injected into one of the tributaries of the portal vein and a series of films taken whilst the patient is still on the operating table.

2. **Percutaneous (Splenography)**

   PREPARATION.   The patient should be sedated, and food and fluids restricted for 6 hr prior to examination.

   TECHNIQUE.   Local anaesthesia is used. The operator punctures the spleen between the tenth and eleventh ribs on the left side, using a long needle with a polythene cannula over it. The needle is then removed, leaving the cannula in position. Two ml of the contrast medium are injected and a pilot film taken (which should include the lower oesophagus). If satisfactory, 20 ml of the medium are then injected and a number of films taken with the aid of a rapid serial film change device (rarely performed nowadays).

3. **Percutaneous (Transhepatic).**   The portal venous system is catheterized by transhepatic puncture using a lateral approach. Once an intrahepatic portal branch has been entered, a special guide wire and catheter are used to advance the system into the portal or splenic main branches. Contrast medium is then injected and films taken using a serial changer.

4. **Percutaneous (via the umbilical vein).**   By direct injection of contrast medium, usually in young children.

5. **Arterial Portography.**   The coeliac axis and superior mesenteric arteries are selectively catheterized, using the retrograde femoral technique with pre-shaped catheters, under screen control. Fifty ml or more of contrast medium are injected rapidly, and a film series taken with a rapid changer. Thus additional arterial information is obtained about the liver, spleen, stomach and pancreas, as well as visualization of the whole of the portal venous system with any collaterals.

6. **Transjugular.**   The approach is via the jugular vein and through the liver.

POSTNASAL SPACE.   *See* ADENOIDS.

PREGNANCY.   *To a large extent ultrasonic diagnosis (q.v.) has replaced radiographic methods in pregnancy as ultrasound waves are generally regarded as safer for the fetus than radiation. But as there are still some cases in which radiography is required, we are therefore retaining this section for reference.*

Prior to the examination the patient should be instructed to empty her bladder and bowel if possible. The radiographer should then ascertain certain facts, if not already given on the request card:

1. Date of last menstrual period (LMP) *or* estimated date of confinement (EDC);
2. Number and details of previous pregnancies;
3. When fetal movements were last felt.

The minimum number of films should be taken to obtain the information required. In most cases an AP supine is the preliminary view.

Anteroposterior Supine. The patient is placed supine with a 35-cm (14-in) linen compression band placed across the abdomen. Firm rigid compression is applied. Centre to the midline at the level of the iliac crests to include the symphysis pubis, maternal pelvis, and as much of the uterus and fetus as possible with a tube–film distance of 90 cm (36 in). The exposure is made on deep inspiration. This film is then processed and examined by the radiologist or experienced radiographer.

Further views are then taken depending on the information required, i.e., whether it is:

1. To demonstrate the fetus; or
2. To measure the maternal pelvis (pelvimetry);

1. *Demonstration of the Fetus.* To determine position, age, multiplicity, and abnormalities. In addition to the AP supine film, a reclining lateral, oblique, or PA view should be taken.

   A. Reclining Lateral. If the fetal spine on the AP film lies to the right of the midline, take a right lateral: if to the left, a left lateral. The patient is placed laterally on the table with her legs extended and shoulders back. A compression band may be used to help her maintain this position. Centre to the centre of the uterus to include the anterior abdominal wall and symphysis pubis.

   B. Oblique. If the fetal spine on the AP film lies to the right of the midline, take a right posterior oblique: if to the left, a left posterior oblique. With the patient supine, rotate her 45° to the required side with legs extended. The under leg is then flexed slightly to maintain the position. Centre to the level of the iliac crest to include the anterior abdominal wall and symphysis pubis.

   C. Postero-anterior. With the patient prone and the wide compression band applied, centre to the midline at the level of the iliac crests to include the symphysis pubis and maternal pelvis. (In this view the patient herself provides a certain amount of compression.)

Note: In doubtful cases of intra-uterine death, an erect AP film may provide confirmatory evidence.

2. *Pelvimetry.* To assess the size and shape of the maternal pelvis as well as any disproportion relative to the fetal head.

A. Anteroposterior Supine. This routine film will already have been taken. The radiographer measures the distance from the table top to the symphysis pubis. The table top to film distance must also be known (this is, of course, constant for each table).

B. Erect Lateral of Pelvis. From this view can be deduced the true conjugate diameter, the mid-pelvic dimensions, and the AP of the outlet. Adjust the film so that its centre is at the mid-pelvis. The intertrochanteric distance is measured using a special calliper (pelvimeter). (From the measurements made on these two films and those obtained by the radiographer, the actual diameters are calculated from a correction chart which allows for the magnification factor.)

C. Outlet. There are no magnification problems here as the patient literally sits on the film! Sitting on the Potter-Bucky table with her feet on the floor and legs wide apart, she bends forward as far as possible. (Most patients should be able to get the spine parallel to the floor.) Centre to the S.2/3 region. This film may be taken with a stationary grid.

Localization of Placental Site. Ultrasonic examination is the method of choice.

PROSTATE. To confirm enlargement of the prostate gland by the demonstration of a filling defect in the base of the bladder.

TECHNIQUE. The bladder is filled with a contrast medium, either as part of an IVP examination, or by carrying out a cystogram. Prostatic enlargement may cause obstruction to the passage of urine, and a large amount of medium remaining in the bladder after micturition provides confirmatory evidence. *Note:* A straight film of the bladder may demonstrate prostatic calculi or a distended bladder.

See BLADDER, CYSTOGRAPHY and INTRAVENOUS UROGRAPHY.

PSOAS MUSCLE. *See* ABDOMEN (Straight).

PUBIS. Two views are usually taken.

1. **Anteroposterior.** With the patient supine on the table, the film is placed transversely under the symphysis pubis to include the pubic bones and the ischium. Centre in the midline to the symphysis pubis.

2. The second view is taken centring to the same position, but with the tube angled 20–25° to the head.

See also SYMPHYSIS PUBIS.

PULMONARY ANGIOGRAPHY. To outline the anatomy of the pulmonary arteries and veins. This is usually performed in cases of pulmonary embolism but may be used to investigate vascular abnormalities in the lungs and mediastinum. Extreme care should be exercised in cases of pulmonary hypertension. The dose of contrast should be reduced by up to one-third in the presence of occlusive pulmonary vascular disease or pulmonary embolic disease. The patient is placed supine over a rapid sequence film changer and a control film taken. A catheter is introduced into the pulmonary artery as for right heart catheter (*see* ANGIOCARDIOGRAPHY). Fifty ml of contrast medium are injected into the main pulmonary artery at 15 ml/sec. Films are then taken at 4 films per sec for 4 sec and then 1 film/sec for up to 9 sec. This is modified as required by the radiologist. Either pulmonary artery can be selectively catheterized and films can then be taken in the PA, lateral or oblique projections. As an alternative to cut films ciné film can be used.

Digital Subtraction Angiography can also be used. A catheter is introduced percutaneously into a vein at the elbow and manipulated into the SVC or right atrium. An initial sequence is taken for the mask. Diluted contrast medium is then injected and subtracted images of the pulmonary vessels are obtained. The length of sequence and rate of acquisition are determined by the radiologist and the condition under consideration. The projections are as above.

PYELOGRAPHY. *See* INTRAVENOUS UROGRAPHY and RETROGRADE shunts, and the diagnosis of pericardial effusions.

RADICULOGRAPHY (LUMBAR). *See* MYELOGRAPHY.

RADIO-ISOTOPE IMAGING. This method depends on the use of radioactive substances which are designed to be taken up by particular organs when introduced into the body, usually intravenously. They emit radiation including γ-rays which can be demonstrated by means of a gamma camera which records activity over the whole field at the same time.

In some organs, such as the brain, a localized area may take up more of the radioactive substance than the surrounding part, producing a 'hot spot' on the scan indicating a tumour or abscess. On the other hand, scanning the lungs, for example, may show a zone of diminished activity suggestive of a pulmonary embolus in cases in which the plain chest radiograph is inconclusive.

A liver scan may show evidence of tumour, abscess, cyst or dilated bile ducts; and a bone scan is a sensitive indicator of secondary deposits in cases of breast and prostatic carcinoma.

Scintigraphy of the heart using radioactive isotopes and a gamma camera can be used in the early detection of myocardial infarct, perfusion of the coronary arteries, studies of the function of the heart muscle, detection and quantification of shunts, and the diagnosis of pericardial effusions.

For fuller details *see* APPENDIX 4.

RADIUS. *See* ELBOW JOINT, FOREARM and WRIST JOINT.

RECTUM. It is usually possible to examine the rectum without recourse to radiography, the notable exception being in the case of newborn infants where it is suspected that there is an imperforate anus. *See* ANAL CANAL.

RENAL ARTERIOGRAPHY. To demonstrate the renal arteries by the injection of a contrast medium.

TECHNIQUE. The method in common use is the retrograde femoral as in AORTOGRAPHY (q.v.) with the tip of the catheter above the level of the renal arteries. Selective injection into the individual arteries is sometimes carried out using a catheter with a curved tip.

RENAL CALCULI (Operative Localization). To demonstrate during operation whether the removal of stones from a kidney has been successful and complete, or the position of those still remaining.

Because the film is placed in an open wound to enable it to lie in contact with the kidney, it must be in a sterile container. A special kidney-shaped film is available from Kodak which is cold sterilized according to the instructions supplied with it.

TECHNIQUE. The kidney is raised by the surgeon by means of a sling. The film is then placed against the kidney and the tube centred from a position anterior to the bony pelvis. Care must be taken not to project the iliac crest on to the film. Rapid processing is essential.

RENAL PUNCTURE. To confirm the presence of a suspected simple renal cyst.

TECHNIQUE. If required to obtain fluid from the cyst, the puncture is made under local anaesthesia using ultrasound to guide the needle.

RENAL TRACT. *See* URINARY TRACT.

RENOGRAPHY. *See* RADIO-ISOTOPE IMAGING and APPENDIX 4.

RETROGRADE PYELOGRAPHY. To demonstrate the kidneys and ureters. This usually follows intravenous urography and may provide additional information in cases of doubtful lesions.

TECHNIQUE. In the operating theatre a fine ureteric catheter is introduced via the urethra and bladder into the ureteric orifice of the side under investigation. Then, either in theatre or the X-ray department, a straight film is taken to ascertain the level of the catheter. If this is in a satisfactory position 5–10 ml of the contrast medium are introduced up the catheter by the doctor. Films are taken immediately in the AP position. Lateral and oblique views may also be taken, and these will usually necessitate a further injection of the medium. Alternatively, the examination may be carried out under screen control.

Note: The procedure is commonly performed with the patient in the Trendelenburg position.

RIBS. For radiographic purposes ribs are divided into upper and lower; the upper being those above the diaphragm and the lower those below. The upper ribs require considerably less exposure than the lower (because the rays pass through the air-filled chest), and it is usually impossible to demonstrate both upper and lower adequately on the same film.

TECHNIQUE. AP (or PA) and oblique views should be taken.

1. Upper Ribs

A. Anteroposterior. Patient erect or supine in the true AP position, the affected side being placed against the film and the central ray directed to the level of the sternal angle. This will enable the maximum number of ribs to be shown above the diaphragm. The film is taken in full inspiration.

B. Postero-anterior. Patient erect or prone, in the true PA position, with the affected side against the film. Centre to the middle of the film in full inspiration.

C. Oblique. Posterior oblique views are usually taken as this enables the side under examination to be placed in contact with the film. Patient erect or supine rotated 45° to the affected side, with the arm of the affected side placed on the head to keep the humerus and shoulder as much out of the way as possible. Centre to the middle of the film.

2. Lower Ribs

A. **Anteroposterior.** Patient supine. If both sides are under examination, a film is placed transversely, with its lower border just below the lower costal margin. Centre to the midline at the level of the lower costal margin and then angle the tube 10° to the patient's head. This will show the maximum number of ribs under the diaphragm. This exposure is made in full expiration. If one side only is under investigation, the patient is moved until that side is over the middle of the table; centre to the midclavicular line at the level of the lower costal margin.

B. **Oblique.** From the above position, the patient is rotated 45° to the affected side. The film is placed with its lower border just below the lower costal margin, with the tube centred to this point. Centre to the midline, then angle the tube 10° to the patient's head. This is to enable the film to be covered with a reasonably small cone without irradiating all the lower abdomen.

SACRO-ILIAC JOINTS

1. **Anteroposterior.** Patient supine. Centre to the midline, about 5 cm (2 in) above the symphysis pubis, with the tube angled 15° to the patient's head. This view will demonstrate both sacro-iliac joints.

2. **Oblique.** The patient is rotated approximately 15–25° to either side in turn. Centre 2·5 cm (1 in) medial to the anterior-superior iliac spine with the central ray perpendicular to the film. *Note:* This view demonstrates the sacro-iliac joint *away* from the film. Both sides are always taken for comparison.

3. **Postero-anterior.** Patient prone. Centre in the midline to the mid-sacral region with the tube angled 10° towards the feet. *Note:* In some centres this view is considered preferable to the anteroposterior one above.

SACRUM

1. **Anteroposterior.** Patient supine. Centre to the midline, approximately 5 cm (2 in) above the symphysis pubis, with the central ray directed 15° to the head.

2. **Lateral.** The patient is rotated into the true lateral position so that the sacrum is approximately over the centre of the table. In this position the sacrum lies rather obliquely, the upper end being considerably further forward than the sacrococcygeal junction which may be felt between the buttocks. It is usually necessary to place a soft wool pad under the mid-lumbar region to straighten the vertebral

column and enable the lumbosacral articulation to be demonstrated on the film. The knees are flexed to give the patient stability. Centre midway between the posterior superior iliac spine and the sacrococcygeal junction.

SALIVARY GLANDS. See PAROTID GLAND, SIALOGRAPHY, SUBLINGUAL GLAND and SUBMANDIBULAR GLAND.

SCAPHOID. PA and oblique views should be taken with ulnar deviation of the hand, together with a lateral. For positioning, *see* WRIST JOINT.

SCAPULA
1. **Anteroposterior.** Patient supine or erect and slightly rotated to bring the scapula of the affected side parallel to the film. Centre over the head of the humerus. (This centring position is used to help project the thoracic cage away from the scapula.)
2. **Lateral.** Patient prone or erect in the anterior oblique position (rotated about 50° from the PA position) with the shoulder of the affected side against the film, and the arm abducted slightly away from the body to prevent the humerus overshadowing the scapula. Centre to the medial border of the scapula. (For this position the arm may be abducted across the body, but in this case the rotation of the body will only need to be about 30°.)
   Note: A supero-inferior view may also be useful, especially when the coracoid process is suspect, but it may be impossible to obtain this view in cases of gross injury. For positioning, *see* SHOULDER JOINT.

SELLA TURCICA. *See* PITUITARY FOSSA.

SHOULDER JOINT
1. **Anteroposterior.** Patient supine or erect and slightly rotated to the affected side. (The opposite side is supported on pads when the supine position is used.) The arm should be extended and the hand rotated outwards so that the palm is facing the tube. Centre to the coracoid process. (For a clear view of the shoulder joint the patient should be further rotated to about 45°, but the resulting picture will not give a satisfactory view of the outer end of the clavicle.)
2. **Lateral Head of Humerus.** From the previous position, the arm is adducted across the chest with the elbow flexed, and the forearm supported by the other hand. This, however, is impossible in the case of injury, and the patient should on

no account be forced into this position. An alternative view (transthoracic) may be obtained as follows:

Patient erect in the true lateral position with the affected side against the film. The opposite arm is lifted out of the way and supported on the patient's head. Centre through the thorax to the head of the humerus against the film.

3. **Supero-inferior.**   Patient seated beside the table. The arm is abducted and rested on a curved cassette, which is tucked well up into the axilla. Centre to the head of the humerus, the central ray being adjusted so that the joint will be projected on to the film.

4. **Inferosuperior.**   This view will give similar results to the super-inferior, and is preferable because the resulting film will not suffer from the distortion present when the curved cassette is used. With the patient supine, the arm is abducted until it is at right-angles to the body. The film is supported vertically against the upper border of the shoulder, and pressed well into the neck. Centre to the head of the humerus, the central ray being as nearly at right-angles to the film as possible.

SHUNTOGRAM.   *See* VENTRICULOGRAPHY.

SIALOGRAPHY.   To demonstrate the salivary glands (sub-mandibular and parotid) and calculi in their ducts.

TECHNIQUE.   Plain films are first taken of the area under review to determine the presence of calculi and calcified cervical glands. (For positioning, *see* PAROTID GLAND and SUB-MANDIBULAR GLAND.)

A 2-ml syringe is used, fitted with a fine catheter. Mouth wash or lemon-juice may be used to promote salivation and thus identify the orifice of the duct. The catheter is carefully inserted and 1–2 ml of the contrast medium are injected and the orifice swabbed. Radiographs are then taken as follows:

1. **Parotid**
   A. Lateral
   B. Postero-anterior
2. **Submandibular**
   A. Lateral oblique
   B. Inferosuperior (occlusal)

SINOGRAPHY.   To demonstrate the extent and direction of sinuses, and their possible connections with internal organs.

TECHNIQUE.   A few ml of the contrast medium are injected, preferably under screen control, and films are taken, usually in the AP and lateral planes.

SINUSES. To demonstrate pathology of the accessory nasal sinuses.

TECHNIQUE. All views should be taken in the erect position, to enable any fluid levels to be demonstrated adequately.

1. **Occipitomental** (maxillary and frontal sinuses). Head in the PA position with the median-sagittal plane at right-angles to the film, and the radiographic base-line tilted up 45° to the horizontal. This will usually mean that the tip of the nose is about 1 cm (½ in) from the film. Centre to the midline at the level of the inferior orbital margin. (If a fluid level is suspected on this film, a second view may be taken with the head in a similar position but flexed 25–30° to the affected side.)

2. **20° Occipitofrontal (inclined posteroanterior)** (frontal and anterior ethmoid sinuses). Head in the PA position, with the median-sagittal plane and the radiographic base-line perpendicular to the film. Centre to the midline at the level of the interorbital line, with the central ray angled 20° to the feet.

3. **Lateral** (all sinuses). Head in the true lateral position with the median-sagittal plane parallel to the film, and the interorbital line perpendicular to the film. Centre 2·5 cm (1 in) behind the outer canthus of the eye.

4. **Oblique** (posterior ethmoid sinuses). The head is placed with the nose, forehead and cheek resting on the table. The median-sagittal plane is 40° to the perpendicular and the radiographic base-line is 30° to the perpendicular. Centre through the orbit in contact with the film. Both sides are taken in turn.

5. **Occipitomental with open mouth** (to demonstrate the sphenoidal sinuses). Head in the PA position with the chin resting on the film. The radiographic base-line is adjusted to 45° from the horizontal. Centre through the open mouth, with the tube angled 25° towards the feet.

SKULL. To demonstrate fractures, bony pathology, and intra-cranial calcification.

The following aids to radiographic positioning are recommended by the Problem Commission on Neuroradiology of the World Federation of Neurology:

The median-sagittal plane. This is the plane which divides the skull symmetrically in half.

The orbital-meatal line. This joins the outer canthus of the eye to the central point of the external auditory meatus. It is often referred to as the Radiographic Base-line, and is used as such throughout this book.

The anthropological base-line. This joins the infraorbital point to the superior border of the external auditory meatus. This is sometimes known as Reid's Base-line.

The interorbital or interpupillary line. This joins the centre of the two orbits or the two pupils. It is perpendicular to the median-sagittal plane.

TECHNIQUE. For routine requests, a 20° occipitofrontal, a 35° fronto-occipital (Townes), and one or both laterals are usually required. All views may be taken erect or lying down. The alternative names given in brackets are those recommended by the Problem Commission.

1. **20° Occipitofrontal (Inclined posteroanterior).** Head in the true PA position with the median-sagittal plane and the radiographic base-line perpendicular to the film. Centre in the midline to the interorbital line, with the central ray angled 20° to the feet.

2. **35° Fronto-occipital (Anteroposterior half axial).** Head in the true AP position with the median-sagittal plane and the radiographic base-line perpendicular to the film. Centre 5 cm (2 in) above the bridge of the nose, with the central ray angled 35° to the feet.

3. **Lateral.** Head in the true lateral position with the median-sagittal plane parallel to the film, and the inter-orbital line perpendicular to the film. Centre 2·5 cm (1 in) above the external auditory meatus. (In the case of injury to the frontal region, it may be advisable to take this view with a horizontal beam and the patient supine, to demonstrate the presence of air in the cranial cavity.)

4. **Submentovertical (Axial).** The neck is hyperextended so that the vertex rests on the film. Support is given to the shoulders before tilting the head back. The median-sagittal plane is perpendicular to the film, and the radiographic base-line is as nearly parallel to the film as possible. Centre to the midline between the angles of the jaw, the central ray being 100° to the radiographic base-line.

   Note: This view (which shows the base of the skull) is easier to take in the erect position, but if it must be taken with the patient supine, the shoulders should be well raised on pillows or sand-bags. A pillow under the buttocks may also help.

5. **10° Fronto-occipital (Inclined anteroposterior).** This view may be taken when other injury prevents the patient from being turned to the prone position for the 20° occipito-frontal view. Head in the true AP position with the

median-sagittal plane and the radiographic base-line
perpendicular to the film. Centre to the bridge of the nose,
the central ray being tilted 10° to the feet.

See also CRIBRIFORM PLATE, FACIAL BONES, MAXILLA, NASAL
BONES, PETROUS TEMPORAL BONES, ZYGOMA and APPENDIX 5
(NAMED VIEWS OF THE SKULL).

SMALL BOWEL ENEMA. *See* BARIUM MEAL (SMALL INTESTINE).

SPHENOIDAL SINUSES. *See* SINUSES.

SPINAL ARTERIOGRAPHY. To demonstrate arteriovenous
malformations of the cord suspected on myelography.

TECHNIQUE. An appropriately shaped catheter is introduced
into the aorta from the femoral artery and manipulated into
the origins of the many segmental spinal branches (which
arise in pairs from the posterior aspect of the thoracic and
lumbar aorta) under direct visualization with an image
intensifier. A short series of films is taken for each branch.

SPINAL VENOGRAPHY. To demonstrate a prolapsed intervertebral disk, especially a lateral protrusion, in cases where one
is still suspected clinically despite a negative radiculogram, by
outlining the veins within the spinal canal.

TECHNIQUE. The ascending lumbar vein is catheterized via the
femoral vein under local anaesthesia and contrast medium
injected. Films are taken using a serial changer.

SPLENOGRAPHY. *See* PORTAL VENOGRAPHY.

STERNOCLAVICULAR JOINT. To demonstrate subluxation
of the sternoclavicular joint, or pathology of the medial end of
the clavicle.

TECHNIQUE

1. **Anteroposterior.** Patient erect, both arms hanging
loosely by the side. Centre to the manubrium sterni. (This
view demonstrates both sides on the one film and is useful
for demonstrating a dislocation.)
2. **Postero-anterior Oblique.** Patient erect or prone in the
PA position. He is then rotated approximately 45° so that
the side under examination is nearest the film. Centre to
the sternoclavicular joint in contact with the film. Both
sides are taken for comparison.
3. **Lateral.** Patient erect in the true lateral position, hands
clasped behind the back and the shoulders drawn well back.

Centre through the sternoclavicular joint, using an anode–
film distance of 150–180 cm (5–6 ft) to compensate for the
increased subject–film distance.

STERNUM

1. **Postero-anterior Oblique.** Patient erect or prone in the PA
   position. He is then rotated to either side approximately 30°.
   Centre to the mid sternal region.
2. **Postero-anterior.** Patient in the true PA position. Centre
   to the level of the axilla 7·5–10·0 cm (3–4 in) lateral to the
   spine, with the tube angled 30° towards the midline. The film
   may be taken during gentle respiration.

   Note: This view cannot normally be taken using the Potter-
   Bucky table, because the grid lines run parallel to the long
   axis of the table, and so would prevent this oblique
   radiation from reaching the film. Because of this difficulty
   this view is usually taken without a grid.

   Alternatively, stand the patient at the side of the table,
   leaning across so that the sternum is resting on it and at
   right-angles to its midline. Centre to the sternum, with the
   tube angled 30° towards the midline. In this position the grid
   may be used.
3. **Lateral.** Patient erect in the true lateral position, with the
   hands clasped behind the back and the shoulders drawn well
   back. Centre to the sternal angle, with an anode–film distance
   of 150–180 cm (5–6 ft) to compensate for the increased
   subject–film distance.

STOMACH. *See* BARIUM MEAL.

SUBLINGUAL GLAND. To demonstrate stones in the glands or
ducts.

TECHNIQUE. One view is usually adequate:

Inferosuperior. An occlusal film is placed transversely in the
mouth, and held gently with the teeth. The head is tilted
back, and the tube centred at right-angles to the film.

SUBMANDIBULAR (SUBMAXILLARY) GLAND. To demon-
strate stones or abnormal calcification in the gland or duct.

TECHNIQUE

1. **Inferosuperior.** An occlusal film is placed in the mouth
   well over to the side under examination, and as far back as
   possible. The head is tilted back, and the tube centred at
   right-angles to the film.
2. **Lateral.** Patient erect or prone with the head in the true

lateral position. A cotton-wool pad placed under the tongue and depressed by the patient will help to bring an opacity below the outline of the jaw. Centre to the angle of the jaw.

3. **Lateral Oblique.** This view is most easily taken in the erect position. Patient seated with the head and body in a true lateral position relative to the tube, which is centred to the angle of the jaw. The patient then holds a film against the side of the face, and the head and film are turned together away from the tube.

See also SIALOGRAPHY.

SUBPHRENIC ABSCESS. An abscess under the diaphragm may give rise to impaired movement of the diaphragm on that side, which is best shown on screen examination. Alternatively films may be taken to demonstrate the amount of movement on both sides during respiration. Sometimes a fluid level may be shown in the abscess. Where available, ultrasound examination is the method of choice. If not, the following views are advised:

1. **Double Diaphragm View.** For this two exposures are made on the same film, one on full expiration, the other on full inspiration. Patient erect, in position as for PA chest. The film is placed transversely, the upper border at the level of the axilla. The first exposure is made on full expiration, using the factors one would use for a PA chest on the same patient. A second exposure is then made on full inspiration, using half the exposure of the former. (The patient should be told what is expected of him before the exposures are made, so that he will not move his position until the two exposures are completed.)

2. **Upper Abdomen.** If the right side is suspect, the patient should be placed erect in an AP position with the lower border of the film at the level of the iliac crest, so as to include the right diaphragm. An exposure is made on expiration. If the left side is suspect, the same positioning can be used with the left side against the film. Lateral views may provide additional information.

SUBTALOID JOINT. The subtaloid joint is the articulation between the calcaneum and the talus, which permits rotation of the foot about its axis.

TECHNIQUE

1. **Lateral.** Patient seated on the table with the leg rotated outwards so that the foot rests on its lateral border

A sand-bag is placed under the knee. Centre to the medial malleolus.

2. **Internal Oblique.** Patient seated, with the leg extended, and the plantar surface of the foot at right-angles to the film. The leg and foot are then rotated inwards until the foot is 45° to the film. Centre 2·5 cm (1 in) below the lateral malleolus with the central ray angled 15° to the head. Other degrees of tube angulation will be required to demonstrate all the articular surfaces. Films taken with 10°, 20°, 30° and 40° tube angulation are required for complete coverage.

3. **External Oblique.** As for the above, but with the leg rotated outwards 45°. Centre 2·5 cm (1 in) below the medial malleolus, again with a tube-tilt of 15° to the head.

SUPRARENAL GLANDS. *See* ADRENAL GLANDS.

SYMPHYSIS MENTI.
To demonstrate fractures or pathology of the anterior arch of the mandible.

TECHNIQUE

1. **Postero-anterior.** Patient erect or prone, with the head in the true PA position, the base-line at right-angles to the film. The head is then rotated 20° to one side, to project the cervical vertebrae clear of the symphysis menti. Centre through the symphysis.

2. **Inferosuperior.** Patient seated or supine. An occlusal film is placed in the mouth, and held gently with the teeth. To demonstrate the bony detail and the lower incisor region generally, the tube is angled 45° to the film. If there is a fracture, another film with the tube at right-angles to it will indicate any displacement present.

Note: These views are meant to supplement the general views of the mandible (q.v.). *See also* TEETH.

SYMPHYSIS PUBIS.
To demonstrate bony pathology, or subluxation of the symphysis pubis.

TECHNIQUE

Anteroposterior. If a fracture or other bony pathology is suspected, with the patient supine centre to the symphysis pubis, the tube tilted 5° to the head. If a subluxation is suspected, two films should be taken in the erect position, the patient slightly lifting first one leg off the ground, then the other.

See also PUBIS.

TALUS. *See* FOOT and SUBTALOID JOINT.

TARSUS (Tarsal Bones). *See* FOOT.

TEETH. Radiography of teeth may be undertaken either intra-
or extra-orally. Under most conditions intra-oral films are the
most satisfactory, because of the proximity of the film to the
tooth under examination, but it should be borne in mind that
any tooth may be demonstrated on an extra-oral film even when
the patient's condition precludes the insertion of a film into the
mouth.

Before commencing the examination, the existing teeth in
the mouth should be charted to give the radiologist a guide.
With intra-oral work, care must be taken with the positioning of
the film in the mouth, and especially the position of the 'dot' on
the corner of the film itself. It should be made a strict rule to
adopt one of two positions and to ensure that all films taken
conform to this. *Either* the 'dot' should be placed to the crown
of the tooth, *or* towards the patient's feet. In the latter case it
will be obvious that a film with the 'dot' to the crown must be of
an upper tooth, and one with the 'dot' towards the roots must be
of a lower tooth, but whichever method is chosen, it should
be adhered to rigidly.

TECHNIQUE

1. **Intra-oral.** The film is placed in the mouth against the
   tooth in question, and the central ray directed so that it is
   at right-angles to the line bisecting the plane of the tooth
   and the plane of the film. The following tube angulations
   are given as an approximate guide, and are relative to the
   occlusal plane:

Upper	Molars	30°	⎫
	Premolars	40°	⎬ Downwards
	Canine	50°	⎪
	Incisors	60°	⎭
Lower	Molars	0–5°	⎫
	Premolars	10–15°	⎬ Upwards
	Canine	25°	⎪
	Incisors	30°	⎭

2. **Extra-oral.** For the molar region the film may be taken
   as for the oblique mandible. For the premolar region the
   head is rotated forward on to the film. For the canine and
   incisor regions, it is easiest to rest the film on the table and
   bend the patient's head over it, the head being slightly
   rotated to the affected side to prevent the cervical spine
   from being superimposed on the teeth. Centre just behind
   angle of jaw away from the film.

See also ORTHOPANTOMOGRAPHY and PANAGRAPHY.

TEMPORAL BONE. *See* PETROUS TEMPORAL BONE and SKULL.

TEMPOROMANDIBULAR JOINTS. To demonstrate the articulations between the condyles of the mandible and the temporal bones. For this examination it is advisable to allow wearers of dentures to keep them in situ, so that when the patient is instructed to close the mouth, a false position is not obtained. Both sides should always be taken for comparison.

TECHNIQUE

1. **Lateral Oblique.** Patient erect or prone with the head in the true lateral position, with the median-sagittal plane parallel to the film, and the interorbital line perpendicular to the film. Centre 5 cm (2 in) above the external auditory meatus away from the film, the central ray being angled 25° to the feet. (Two views are taken for each side, mouth open and mouth closed. For the former the patient is instructed to keep the back teeth together.)

2. **35° Fronto-occipital.** Patient supine or erect with the head in the true AP position and the median-sagittal plane and radiographic base-line perpendicular to the film. Centre to the midline with the tube tilted 35° to the feet, so that the central ray passes midway between the external auditory meatuses. *Note:* The film will require considerable displacement downwards to prevent the joint being projected off the film. (This view shows the condylar heads when the mouth is open.)

3. **Tomography.** Tomography may be very useful. Films are taken with the head in the true lateral position, a 15–20° angle cut usually proving quite satisfactory.

THERMOGRAPHY. Infrared radiation is given off continuously by one's skin, and this can be converted by an infrared camera into an image which is displayed on a cathode-ray tube. Basically it detects alterations in skin temperature, for instance, increased temperature in breast tumours producing higher infrared emissions.

THORACIC INLET. To demonstrate deviation or compression of the trachea.

TECHNIQUE

1. **Anteroposterior.** Patient supine or erect in the true AP position with the chin raised. Centre to the sternal notch.

2. **Lateral.** Patient erect, hands clasped behind the back,

and shoulders forced as far back as possible. Centre to the sternal notch, using an anode–film distance of 150–180 cm (5–6 ft). (It will help to explain beforehand to the patient that the success of this view depends entirely on how much the shoulders can be held back. Because it may be difficult to sustain this position, the patient should not be asked to adopt it until the radiographer is ready to make the exposure.)

3. **Oblique.** This view will show the trachea from larynx to carina. Patient erect, facing the tube. The body is then rotated 45° to either side in turn. Centre to the mid-point of the clavicle nearest the tube.

THORACIC VERTEBRAE

1. **Anteroposterior.** Patient supine. Centre to the midline approximately 2·5 cm (1 in) below the sternal angle.

2. **Oblique.** From the AP position the patient is rotated 45° to each side in turn, being supported in this position by means of non-opaque pads under the hips and the shoulders. Centre to the midclavicular line nearest the tube, at the level of 2·5 cm (1 in) below the sternal angle.

3. **Lateral.** Patient in the true lateral position, hands on the pillow in front of his head, knees flexed to help maintain balance. If the spinous processes of the vertebrae are palpated, their general alignment relative to the table top may be felt, and by inserting non-opaque pads under the lower ribs it should be possible to position the vertebral column parallel to the film. Centre through the axilla 2·5 cm (1 in) below the level of the sternal angle. (An alternative to this may be taken with the patient erect as for a lateral chest, using 150 cm (5 ft) FFD.)

4. **Lateral (T.1–T.3).** This region is not usually demonstrated on the general lateral film because of the superimposition of the shoulders. There are many methods used to attempt to overcome this, for example:

   A. From the above lateral position, the arm nearest the tube is brought back and the hand rested on the table behind the patient. Centre just anterior to the shoulder away from the film, the tube being tilted 10° to the head.

   B. With the patient erect in the true lateral position, both arms and shoulders are brought as far forward as possible and the chin tucked well down to the chest. Centre to the spinous process of C.7. (If a high kV can be used for this exposure, it may be possible to demonstrate the vertebrae from C.3 to T.5 on the one film.)

THORACOLUMBAR JUNCTION

1. **Anteroposterior.** Patient supine. Centre to the midline at the level of L.1.
2. **Lateral.** Patient in the true lateral position. Centre to L.1. (Two films may be used together in a single cassette which contains two pairs of specially graded screens of different speeds. Thus one film shows clearly the lower thoracic vertebrae and the other the upper lumbar.)

THUMB. *Note:* The thumb extends from the base of the first metacarpal, and it is essential to ensure that this is included on the film.

1. **Anteroposterior.** Patient seated or kneeling, the arm extended along the table, palm down and elbow straight. From this position the hand is rotated inwards with the thumb down until it is in the AP position. Centre to the metacarpophalangeal joint.
2. **Lateral.** Patient seated, hand relaxed in the PA position, with the thumb resting on the film, the hand supported on a non-opaque pad. Centre to the metacarpophalangeal joint.
3. **Postero-anterior.** This position may be used as an alternative to the AP position in the case of injury making that position difficult to obtain. Patient seated with the hand in the true lateral position, thumb extended and resting on a non-opaque pad. Centre to the metacarpophalangeal joint.

See also HAND.

THYMUS. To demonstrate abnormal enlargement of the thymus gland.

TECHNIQUE. PA and lateral views are taken as for the chest; care being taken to ensure accurate positioning, especially of the head and neck in relation to the body. For the lateral view the hands should be held behind the back, with the shoulders well back.

Note: In children, the thymus is most clearly shown when they are crying.

Where available, computerized tomography may provide additional information.

TIBIA

1. **Anteroposterior.** Patient seated with the leg extended, foot upright and the knee in the true AP position. Centre to the middle of the lower leg. (It should be possible to include the knee joint and ankle joint on the one film, but if not, the joint nearest the site of injury should be included.)

2. Lateral. From the AP position the patient is rotated on to the affected side, with the leg resting on the film. Centre to the middle of the lower leg.

See also ANKLE JOINT, FIBULA and KNEE JOINT.

TOES. *See* FOOT.

TOMOGRAPHY. It is only intended to discuss the technique of tomography so far as it concerns the radiographer undertaking the examination. For the physical principles the radiographer is referred to one of the many textbooks that deal with the subject.

Two methods are in use:

1. **Sequential (One Film at a Time).** The cut required is set by moving the pivot (fulcrum) up or down and reading the level off the scale attached to a pivot.

2. **Multisection (more than One Film per Exposure: Usually 3, 5 or 7).** The scale reading should be set at the level of the top cut required. This will be recorded on the top film in the cassette, the films beneath giving predetermined sections below this. (It should be remembered when unloading the cassette that, since most cassettes load from the bottom, the last film out will be the top cut.) For this work the screens are carefully graded to give even densities throughout the films, and care should be taken not to alter their order in the cassette.

It is generally accepted that with these multiple film techniques, definition will be lower than with sequential tomography. Furthermore, for the films to be of comparable density the range of kV that can be used is strictly limited to between 75 and 90. Even reducing this to 70 kV will make the top film appreciably darker than the bottom. It will also be necessary to increase the exposure, at approximately the following rates:

    3-film cassette   × 2 of the sequential
    5-film cassette   × 3 of the sequential
    7-film cassette   × 5 of the sequential

Note: **Angle of Movement.** The angle that the tube moves about the pivot determines the thickness of the cut that has acceptable definition, and the following is suggested as a guide:

20° arc gives 1 cm thick cut for vertebral bodies and temporomandibular joints.

30° arc give 4 mm thick cut for routine chest work.

50° arc gives 1·2 mm thick cut for inner and middle ear structures, optical canals, etc.

If it is not possible to adjust the angle of movement to as small as 20°, it may be possible to arrange that the timer terminates the exposure when the tube is roughly at the middle of its travel, thus giving about half the set angle.

See also COMPUTERIZED TOMOGRAPHY and ZONOGRAPHY.

TRACHEA. *See* CHEST and THORACIC INLET.

TRAPEZIUM. *See* WRIST JOINT.

TRAPEZOID. *See* WRIST JOINT.

TRIQUETRUM. *See* WRIST JOINT.

ULNA. *See* ELBOW JOINT, FOREARM and WRIST JOINT.

ULNAR GROOVE. *See* ELBOW JOINT.

ULTRASOUND IMAGING. Ultrasonic waves have a frequency far higher than can be recorded by the human ear and when directed at the body, travel through it at the rate of about 1500 m/sec. When, however, they reach a surface with a different texture, a wave is reflected back from the surface of the object which can be amplified and displayed on a cathode ray tube, and a photograph taken as a permanent record if required. The image is displayed in various shades of grey (grey scale) according to the echo strength, rather than just black and white, thus making interpretation easier.

It is an easily performed technique, once the operator has been trained; it is non-invasive, has no known side-effects and it can be repeated as required.

The principal uses are in:

Obstetrics—to assess early pregnancy (6–8 weeks); fetal growth; fetal abnormalities, such as spina bifida, anencephaly and cardiac malformations; and to detect placenta praevia.

Liver disease—to assess whether jaundice is obstructive or non-obstructive by the demonstration of dilated ducts within the liver. Tumours, cysts and abscesses can be visualized. Calculi in the bile ducts and in the gallbladder are easily identified.

Abdomen—cysts and tumours can be distinguished, e.g. in the pancreas and kidneys. The aorta can be visualized and aneurysms demonstrated. The adrenal glands and aortic lymph nodes are other organs well shown by this method.

Cardiology (echocardiography)—to study in particular the

shape and movement of heart valves; to detect early pericardial effusions; and to assess congenital heart disease and cardiomyopathies. Usually carried out in specialized cardiac centres. Almost eliminates the need for invasive techniques in children.

ULTRASONIC DOPPLER. This technique utilizes the Doppler effect which arises when continuous ultrasonic waves reflect off moving objects, to give an audible indication of the rate of movement of the object. Initially it was used to listen to fetal hearts in utero, but it is now used also to determine blood flow in arteries and veins, where it can give an indication of the state of the arteries or the possibility of deep vein thrombosis.

UPPER JAW. *See* MAXILLA.

URETERS. *See* INTRAVENOUS UROGRAPHY, RETROGRADE PYELOGRAPHY and URINARY TRACT.

URETHRA AND URETHROGRAPHY. *See* CYSTO-URETHROGRAPHY.

URINARY TRACT. To demonstrate radiopaque calculi, or abnormal calcification.

TECHNIQUE. For plain radiography two views are usually taken: (1) from the upper pole of the kidneys down to the lower end of the sacro-iliac joints, and (2) a bladder film.

1. **Anteroposterior.** Patient supine. Centre to the midline at the level of the lower costal margin.

2. **Bladder Film.** Patient supine. Centre to the midline approximately 7·5 cm (3 in) above the symphysis pubis, with 20° tilt to the feet.

If a stone is suspected to be in the kidney on the straight film, separate inspiration and expiration films of this area should be taken. These will demonstrate whether or not the stone keeps a constant relationship to the kidney during the two phases of respiration. IVU examination will provide confirmatory evidence.

If the stone is suspected to be in the ureter, IVU examination may be carried out; or a retrograde catheter passed, and straight and oblique views taken to demonstrate the relationship of the suspected stone to the path of the ureter.

See also INTRAVENOUS UROGRAPHY and RETROGRADE PYELOGRAPHY.

UTEROSALPINGOGRAPHY. *See* HYSTEROSALPINGOGRAPHY.

VENOGRAPHY. To demonstrate the patency of the deep veins of the leg, pelvis, or axilla.

TECHNIQUE

Leg. A number of techniques are in use, the simplest involving the injection of at least 50 ml of a dilute contrast medium into a superficial vein on the dorsum of the foot by means of a flexible plastic catheter, while a tourniquet is applied above the tip of the catheter to occlude the superficial circulation.

An AP film of the lower leg is taken 5–10 sec after the injection; and of the upper leg (thigh region) approximately 20 sec later. If desired, lateral films may be obtained in a similar fashion following the injection of a further 20 ml of the contrast medium.

Alternatively, contrast medium from a drip infusion bottle may be used for continuous perfusion of the veins, and films taken under screen control.

Pelvis. The contrast medium is injected directly into the femoral vein and films taken of the iliac veins at approximately 1-sec intervals for 5 sec. A further injection may be needed with a tourniquet on the lower leg.

Axilla. The contrast medium is injected directly into the median cubital vein and films taken of the axillary region at approximately 1 sec intervals for 5 sec.

Other techniques include the retrograde femoral and intraosseous methods, for details of which reference should be made to larger textbooks. Superficial venography may also be carried out to demonstrate the superficial veins of the legs, adrenals, pancreas, parathyroids and testicles.

See also ULTRASONIC DOPPLER.

VENTRICULOGRAPHY. To demonstrate the ventricles of the brain by the direct injection of air or a positive contrast medium.

This examination is rarely used now, except as a way of testing patency of shunt tubes which have been inserted in a lateral ventricle and so is often referred to as a 'Shuntogram'. Non-ionic contrast media are used which mix with CSF and are soon absorbed.

VERTEBRAL ANGIOGRAPHY. *See* CEREBRAL ANGIOGRAPHY.

VESICULOGRAPHY. To demonstrate the vas deferens and seminal vesicle by the use of a contrast medium.

TECHNIQUE. Under local anaesthesia, a small incision is made in the inguinal region and the vas deferens exposed. A few ml of the contrast medium are then injected, and straight films taken. (This procedure is rarely used.)

VOCAL CORDS. *See* LARYNX.

WRIST JOINT
  1. **Postero-anterior.** Patient seated with the forearm resting on the table, palm downwards, fingers flexed to bring the wrist in contact with the film. Centre midway between the ulnar and radial styloid processes.
  2. **Lateral.** From the PA position rotate the hand, thumb upwards, until the hand is in the true lateral position. The hand should then be further rotated backwards about 10° to superimpose the radius on the ulna. Centre to the radial styloid process.
  3. **Oblique 1.** From the PA position rotate the hand 45° towards the lateral position. A soft pad should be placed under the thumb to give support to the hand. Centre to the ulnar styloid process.
  4. **Oblique 2.** From the lateral position, further rotate the hand backwards another 45°. Centre to the ulnar styloid process.
     Note: The first oblique view is the more widely used for routine purposes. If the scaphoid is under suspicion, the PA and both oblique views should be taken with ulnar deviation of the hand.
  5. **Inclined Postero-anterior.** Patient seated with the forearm resting on the table, palm downwards, with ulnar deviation. Centre in the midline between the styloid processes with the central ray angled 25° towards the elbow.
  6. **Carpal Tunnel View.** Patient seated beside the table, with the anterior aspect of the lower part of the forearm resting on the edge of the table. The hand and thumb of the side under examination are forced backwards by the patient using the other hand, and the forearm adjusted until it is 45° to the table. This will bring the wrist about 4 in (10 cm) above the table, and enable an inferosuperior view to be taken of its anterior surface without superimposition of the hand. Centre to the mid-palmar region of the hand, with the central ray vertical. *Note:* This view is useful to demonstrate any bony cause of pressure on the nerves of the hand as they pass through the carpal tunnel.
     Note: The following views are recommended:
       Lower end of radius and ulna: PA and lateral.

Scaphoid: PA, obliques 1 and 2 (all with ulnar deviation)
and inclined PA.
Lunate: PA and lateral.
Trapezoid: Oblique 1 with ulnar deviation.
Pisiform: Oblique 2.

XEROGRAPHY. This is a photo-electric method of recording
an image on paper.

In the light-tight conditioner unit, a special reversible plate
(aluminium base with a selenium photo-conductor coating on
one side) is given a positive electrical charge on the surface of
the selenium and then loaded automatically into a cassette.
Radiography is carried out in the usual way.

The plate is then removed automatically from the cassette in
the light-tight developer unit. A blue powder (toner) is blown
onto the selenium surface to visualize the latent image which is
transferred onto paper and fused into it by heating, producing a
permanent blue image. In the latest processor a black toner is
used instead.

Uses:
1. Mammography (q.v.).
2. Other soft tissues.
3. Fractures through plaster.
4. Other procedures such as sialography and peripheral
   angiography.
5. Tomography of mediastinum (usually pre-radiotherapy).
6. Foreign bodies.

ZONOGRAPHY. This is the technique of using a very narrow-
angle tomographic cut, to give a thick section with acceptable
sharpness. It may be used where the structures that are required
to be blurred are an appreciable distance from the area of
interest, e.g. gas in the bowel on an IVU examination, or for
temporomandibular joints. A linear cut of 10°, or a circular cut
of between 3° and 6°, can be used in these circumstances.
See also TOMOGRAPHY.

ZYGOMA and ZYGOMATIC ARCH. These are usually well
shown on occipitomental and 30° occipitomental views (*see*
FACIAL BONES). In addition, to show the arch, a 35° fronto-
occipital (with a reduction in exposure of at least 10 kV from
the normal) and a submentovertical (with a reduction in
exposure of 15–20 kV from the normal) may be found useful.
For positioning, *see* SKULL.

Appendix 1
CONTRAST MEDIA

These tables contain a comprehensive list of contrast media available in the United Kingdom at the time of going to press. They have been compiled from information supplied by the various manufacturers, and reference should ALWAYS be made to their detailed literature before administration.

A. Indications

Indication	*Contrast media*
Abdomen (acute)	Gastrografin
Angiocardiography ⎱ Aortography ⎰	Cardio-Conray
	Conray 280; 325; 420
	Hexabrix
	Hypaque 65%; 85%
	Isopaque 350
	Isopaque Coronar 370
	Niopam 370
	Omnipaque 350
	Urografin 310 M; 370
	Uromiro 380; 420
Arthrography	Conray 280
	Hexabrix
	Hypaque 25%; 45%
	Isopaque Amin 200
	Niopam 300
	Omnipaque 240; 300
	Urografin 310 M
Barium examinations	Baritop 100; G: PLUS
	E-Z-HD
	E-Z-Paque
	Micropaque Standard; DC: HD
	Microtrast
	Polibar
Brachial arteriography	Conray 280
	Hexabrix
	Hypaque 45%
	Isopaque Cerebral 280
	Niopam 300; 370
	Omnipaque 300; 350
	Urografin 310 M
	Uromiro 300; 340; 380

Indication	Contrast media
Bronchography	Dionosil aqueous
	Dionosil oily
	Iodatol
Cerebral angiography	Conray 280
	Hexabrix
	Isopaque Cerebral 280
	Niopam 300
	Omnipaque 300
	Urografin 310 M
	Uromiro 300
Cholangiography (direct)	Biligram
	Conray 280
	Hypaque 25%; 45%
	Urografin 290
	Uromiro 300
Cholecystangiography (i.v.)	Biligram
	Biliscopin
	Endobil
Cholecystography (oral)	Biloptin
	Cistobil
	Solu-biloptin
	Telepaque
Coronary arteriography (*See* Aortography)	
Cysto-urethrography	Hypaque 25%; 45%
	Isopaque Cysto 100
	Lipiodol ultra fluid
	Umbradil viscous U
	Urografin 150 (cystography); 370 (urethrography)
Dacryo-cystography	Hypaque 45%
	Lipiodol ultra fluid
Discography	Conray 280
	Hypaque 45%
Femoral arteriography (*See* Brachial arteriography)	
Hystero-salpingography	Hexabrix
	Hypaque 45%
	Lipiodol ultra fluid
	Urografin 310 M; 370

Indication	*Contrast media*
Intravenous pyelography (urography)	Conray 280; 325; 420
	Hexabrix
	Hypaque 45%
	Isopaque 280; 350; 440
	Niopam 300; 370
	Omnipaque 300; 350
	Sodium Uromiro 300
	Urografin 290; 325; 370
	Uromiro 300; 340; 380; 420
Lymphography	Lipiodol ultra fluid
Myelography	Myodil
	Niopam 200; 300
	Omnipaque 180; 240; 300
Portal venography	Conray 280; 325; 420
	Hexabrix
	Hypaque 45%; 65%; 85%
	Isopaque 370; 440
	Niopam 370
	Urografin 310 м; 370
Radiculography	Niopam 200; 300
	Omnipaque 180; 240
Renal arteriography (*See* Brachial arteriography)	
Retrograde pyelography	Hypaque 25%
	Urografin 150
Sialography	Hypaque 45%; 65%
	Isopaque Coronar 370; 440
	Lipiodol ultra fluid
	Urografin 290
Sinography	Dionosil aqueous
	Hypaque 45%
	Lipiodol ultra fluid
	Urografin 290
Urethrography (*See* Cysto-urethrography)	
Venography	Conray 280; 325; 420
	Hexabrix 200
	Hypaque 45%
	Isopaque Amin 200
	Niopam 300; 370
	Omnipaque 240; 300
	Urografin 310 м; 325
	Uromiro 300; 340

Indication	*Contrast media*
Ventriculography	Myodil
	Niopam 300
Vesiculography	Hypaque 45%
	Lipiodol ultra fluid
	Urografin 370

B. Common or Approved Names

Proprietary name	Common or approved name	Manufacturer	Iodine content (mg/ml)
Baritop (Liquid)	Barium sulphate 100% w/v	Concept Pharmaceuticals	—
Baritop G (Powder)	Barium sulphate		
Baritop Plus (Powder)	Barium sulphate (high density)		
Biligram	Meglumine Ioglycamate	Schering	
	—ampoule 35%		176 mg
	—infusion 17%		85 mg
Biliscopin	Meglumine iotroxinate	Schering	
	—ampoule 38%		180 mg
	—infusion 10·5%		50 mg
Biloptin	Sodium ipodate, 0·5 g capsules	Schering	—
Cardio-Conray	Meglumine and sodium iothalamate	May & Baker	400 mg
Cistobil	Iopanoic acid 0·5 g tablets	Bracco/Merck	—
Conray 280	Meglumine iothalamate B.P. 60%	May & Baker	280 mg
Conray 325	Sodium iothalamate 54%	May & Baker	325 mg
Conray 420	Sodium iothalamate 70%	May & Baker	420 mg
Dionosil aqueous	Propyliodone suspension B.P. 50% aqueous	Glaxo	284 mg
Dionosil oily	Propyliodone suspension B.P. 60% oily	Glaxo	340 mg
Endobil	Meglumine iodoxamate 9-91% (for infusion)	Bracco/Merck	45 mg
E-Z-HD	Barium sulphate 250% w/v	E-Z-Em⁵	—
E-Z-Paque	Barium sulphate 170% w/v	E-Z-Em	—

Proprietary name	Common or approved name	Manufacturer	Iodine content (mg/ml)
Gastrografin	Sodium and meglumine diatrizoate 76% with wetting agent and flavouring	Schering	370 mg
Hexabrix 320	Sodium ioxaglate 19·65% w/v and meglumine ioxaglate 39·3% w/v	May & Baker	320 mg
Hypaque 25%	Sodium diatrizoate B.P. 25%	Sterling	150 mg
Hypaque 45%	Sodium diatrizoate B.P. 45%	Sterling	270 mg
Hypaque 65%	Sodium and meglumine diatrizoate 65%	Sterling	390 mg
Hypaque 85%	Sodium and meglumine diatrizoate 85%	Sterling	440 mg
Isopaque 350	Sodium metrizoate (with calcium, magnesium and meglumine)	Nycomed	350 mg
Isopaque 440	Sodium metrizoate (with calcium, magnesium and meglumine)	Nycomed	440 mg
Isopaque Amin 200	Meglumine and calcium metrizoates	Nycomed	200 mg
Isopaque Cerebral 280	Meglumine and calcium metrizoates	Nycomed	280 mg
Isopaque Coronar 370	Meglumine, sodium and calcium metrizoates	Nycomed	370 mg
Isopaque Cysto 100	Sodium metrizoate (with calcium, magnesium and meglumine)	Nycomed	100 mg
Lipiodol ultra fluid	Iodized ethyl esters of the fatty acids of poppy-seed oil	May & Baker	—
Lipiodol viscous	Iodized oil injection B.P.	May & Baker	—
Micropaque standard	Colloidal barium sulphate 100% w/v	Nicholas	—
Micropaque DC	Barium sulphate 100% w/v	Nicholas	—
Micropaque HD	Barium sulphate 230% w/v	Nicholas	—

Proprietary name	Common or approved name	Manufacturer	Iodine content (mg/ml)
Microtrast	Colloidal barium sulphate paste 70% w/v	Nicholas	—
Myodil	Iophendylate injection B.P.	Glaxo	300 mg
Niopam 200	Iopamidol	Bracco/Merck	200 mg
Niopam 300	Iopamidol	Bracco/Merck	300 mg
Niopam 370	Iopamidol	Bracco/Merck	370 mg
Omnipaque	Iohexol	Nycomed	180 mg
			240 mg
			300 mg
			350 mg
Polibar	Barium sulphate 80% w/v	E-Z-Em	—
Polibar ACB	Barium sulphate 115% w/v	E-Z-Em	—
Sodium Uromiro 300	Sodium iodamide 53%	Bracco/Merck	300 mg
Solu-biloptin	Calcium ipodate., 3 g powder	Schering	—
Telepaque	Iopanoic acid B.P., 0·5 g tablets	Sterling	—
Urografin 150	Sodium and meglumine diatrizoate 30%	Schering	146 mg
Urografin 290	Sodium and meglumine diatrizoate 60%	Schering	292 mg
Urografin 325	Sodium and meglumine diatrizoate 58%	Schering	325 mg
Urografin 370	Sodium and meglumine diatrizoate 76%	Schering	370 mg
Urografin 310 м	Meglumine diatrizoate 65%	Schering	305·8 mg
Uromiro 300	Meglumine iodamide 65%	Bracco/Merck	300 mg
Uromiro 340	Sodium and meglumine iodamide 62%	Bracco/Merck	340 mg
Uromiro 380	Sodium and meglumine iodamide 79%	Bracco/Merck	380 mg
Uromiro 420	Sodium and meglumine iodamide 80%	Bracco/Merck	420 mg

Notes:

1. The products of Nyegaard are distributed in the United Kingdom by Nycomed (UK) Limited.
2. The products of Schering A.G. (Berlin) are distributed in the United Kingdom by Schering Pharmaceuticals.
3. The products of Bracco Chemical Industries (Milan, Italy) are distributed in the United Kingdom by E. Merck Ltd.
4. E-Z-Em products are distributed in the United Kingdom by Henleys Medical Supplies Ltd.
5. Sterling—Sterling Research Laboratories (formerly Winthrop).

Appendix 2

GLOSSARY OF MEDICAL TERMS

Abscess: A cavity which contains pus.

Achalasia: Narrowing of the lower end of the oesophagus due to spasm.

Achondroplasia: Failure of bones to reach normal length because of interference with their ossification during growth.

Acid-fast lesion: Tuberculous disease.

Acoustic neuroma: A benign tumour of the eighth cranial nerve.

Acromegaly: Overgrowth of certain bony structures and soft tissues as a result of a pituitary tumour.

Adamantinoma: A locally malignant tumour of the mandible.

Addison's disease: Defective seretion of the adrenal cortex.

Adenoma: A benign tumour of glandular tissue.

Adhesions: Bands of fibrous tissue in body cavities formed as a result of previous inflammation.

Agenesis: Total failure of development.

Albuminuria: Albumin in the urine.

Amenorrhoea: Absence of menstruation.

Anencephaly: Failure of development of the fetal brain and cranium.

Aneurysm: Localized dilatation of an artery.

Angina pectoris: Chest pain originating in the heart.

Angioma: Benign tumour arising from blood vessels.

Angiosarcoma: Malignant tumour of bone.

Ankylosing spondylitis: Arthritis of the sacro-iliac joints and spine resulting in fusion of vertebrae.

Ankylosis: Fusion of a joint.

Anorexia: Loss of appetite.

Aortic regurgitation: Back-flow through the aortic valve.

Aortic stenosis: Narrowing of the aortic valve.

Arachnodactyly: A condition of elongation of the long bones of the hands and feet.

Arteriosclerosis: Thickening and hardening of arterial walls with narrowing of the lumen.

Arteritis: Inflammation of an artery.

Arthritis: Inflammation of a joint.

Arthrodesis: Surgical fusion of a joint.

Arthroplasty: Formation of an artificial joint.

Asbestosis: Disease of the lung caused by inhalation of asbestos fibres.

Ascites: Excessive fluid in the peritoneal cavity.

Asthma: A disease causing spasm of the muscles in the walls of the smaller bronchi causing breathing difficulties.

Astrocytoma: A type of intracranial neoplasm.

Atelectasis: Pulmonary collapse.

Atheroma: Fatty degeneration of the inner lining of arteries.

Atherosclerosis: A combination of arteriosclerosis and atheroma.

Atresia: Failure of channel formation in the development of hollow organs.

Atrophy: Shrinkage in the size of tissues.

Auricular fibrillation: An abnormality of the rhythm of the heart beat.

Benign: Simple, non-malignant.

Bennett's fracture: Fracture of the base of the first metacarpal.

Bright's disease: A form of nephritis.

Brodie's abscess: An abscess cavity in a bone as a result of osteomyelitis.

Bronchiectasis: Dilatation of the distal bronchi, usually associated with infection.

Bronchitis: Inflammation of the mucosal lining of the bronchi.

Bronchopneumonia: Patchy inflammation of the lung.

Bronchoscopy: Examination of the bronchi by direct visual inspection through a special instrument passed down the trachea.

Bursa: A membranous sac containing a small quantity of fluid to facilitate movement between two adjacent structures.

Bursitis: Inflammation of a bursa.

Caesarean section: Delivery of a fetus through a surgical incision in the abdominal wall.

Calcinosis: Abnormal areas of calcification in the tissues.

Calculus: A stone.

Callus: New bone laid down in the healing of fractures.

Carcinoma: A malignant tumour arising from epithelial tissue.

Carcinomatosis: Widespread small metastases.

Cardiac: Pertaining to the heart.

Cardiospasm: Achalasia (q.v.).

Carditis: Inflammation of the heart.

Cellulitis: Diffuse inflammation of connective tissue.

Cholecystectomy: Surgical removal of the gallbladder.

Cholecystitis: Inflammation of the gallbladder.

Cholelithiasis: The formation of stones in the gallbladder or its ducts.

Cholesteatoma: A tumour-like mass in the middle ear which may erode the bony walls of the middle ear and the mastoid.

Chondroma: A benign tumour of cartilage.

Chondrosarcoma: A malignant tumour of cartilage.

Chordoma: A rare type of malignant neoplasm in the skull or in the sacrococcygeal region.

Chorea (St Vitus's dance): A disease of the nervous system, characterized by involuntary movements.

Cirrhosis: A condition of diffuse necrosis of liver cells and widespread replacement fibrosis in the areas of cell destruction.

Claudication, intermittent: Pain in a limb caused by exertion when there is a defective blood supply.

Cleidocranial dystosis: A condition with defects of bone in the clavicles and skull.

Coarctation: A congenital narrowing in the arch of the aorta.

Colic: Severe abdominal pain of the paroxysmal type.

Colles fracture: A fracture of the lower end of the radius with posterior displacement of the lower fragment.

Colostomy: An artificial opening of the colon on to the anterior abdominal wall.

Congenital: Existing at the time of birth.

Congestion: An accumulation of excessive blood in the body tissues.

Consolidation: Solidification, used especially of lungs which become solid by the collection of exudate in the alveoli.

Contusion: Bruising.

Cor pulmonale: Heart disease, secondary to obstruction in the pulmonary circulation or chronic disease of the lungs.

Coxa vara: Congenital deformity of the hip.

Craniolacuna: Multiple small bony defects in the skull.

Craniostenosis: Premature fusion of some of the cranial sutures.

Crepitations: Moist sounds heard in diseased lungs.

Cretinism: A condition resulting from iodine deficiency or marked under-development of the thyroid gland.

Crohn's disease (regional enteritis): Chronic non-specific inflammation of the intestine.

Cushing's syndrome: Hyperfunction of the adrenal cortex.

Cyanosis: Blueness of the skin caused by insufficient oxygenation.

Cyesis: Pregnancy.

Cyst: A hollow sac containing fluid, semi-solid material or air.

Cystadenoma: A type of neoplasm of the ovaries.

Cysticercosis: A rare disease resulting from ingestion of the eggs of the pork tapeworm.

Cystoscopy: Examination of the bladder visually by means of an instrument passed up the urethra.

Dacryocystitis: Inflammation of the lacrimal sac (tear sac).

Degeneration: Deterioration of tissue to a lower state.

Dementia: A type of mental degeneration characterized by failure or loss of mental powers.

Dermoid cyst: A sac-like structure filled with semi-fluid material and sometimes containing hair, teeth and bone elements.

Diabetes mellitus: A disease characterized by high blood sugar due to deficient production of insulin by the pancreas.

Diaphyseal aclasia (dyschondroplasia): A condition in which multiple small outgrowths (exostoses) arise from bones preformed in cartilage.

Dilatation: abnormal enlargement of an organ due to stretching.

Dislocation: A displacement of one or more bones which form a joint.

Diverticulitis: Inflammation of diverticula of the bowel.

Diverticulosis: The presence of diverticula in the bowel.

Diverticulum (pl. diverticula): A sac or pouch arising from a hollow organ.

Ductus arteriosus, patent: Failure of closure of the ductus arteriosus after birth.

Dyschondroplasia: Diaphyseal aclasia (q.v.).

Dysmenorrhoea: Painful menstrual periods.

Dyspepsia: Indigestion.

Dysphagia: Difficulty in swallowing.

Dysplasia: Defective formation of bone.

Dyspnoea: Difficulty in breathing.

Dystrophy: Abnormal bone formation caused by defective nutrition.

Dysuria: Difficult and/or painful micturition.

Ecchondroma: A benign tumour of cartilage which projects from the outer surface of a bone.

Ectopic pregnancy: Implantation of a fetus outside the uterine cavity, e.g., in the Fallopian tubes.

Effusion: The formation of fluid in a body cavity.

Embolism: Obstruction of an artery by a portion of blood clot or other foreign matter, e.g., fat or hair.

Emphysema (pulmonary): Excessive distension of the lung alveoli due to prolonged strain (e.g., in chronic bronchitis). *See also* Surgical emphysema.

Empyema: A collection of pus in an enclosed cavity, e.g., the pleural cavity.

Encephalitis: Inflammation of the outer lining of the brain.

Enchondroma: A benign tumour of cartilage growing within the interior of a bone.

Endocarditis: Inflammation of the endocardium of the heart.

Enteritis, regional: Crohn's disease (q.v.).

Epilepsy: A disorder of the nervous system characterized by sudden loss of consciousness, sometimes associated with convulsions.

Epistaxis: Nose bleeding.

Epithelioma: Tumour derived from epithelial cells.

Erythema nodosum: An allergic response which gives rise to reddish patches on the shins or forearms.

Erythrocytes: Red blood-cells.

Ewing's tumour: A malignant tumour of bone.

Exacerbation: Increase in severity (of symptoms).

Exophthalmos: Protrusion of the eyeballs.

Exostosis: An outgrowth of bone.

Fibrillation: Rapid fluttering movement of muscle. (Usually used in connection with heart muscle.)

Fibroid (fibromyoma): A simple tumour of the uterus consisting of fibrous and muscle tissue.

Fibrosis: Formation of fibrous tissue.

Fibrositis: A disease of skeletal muscles.

Fissure: A crack or tear.

Fistula: An unnatural communication between two hollow organs, or between one and the surface.

Fits: Usually refers to epilepsy (q.v.).

Fracture: A break in the continuity of a bone.

Freiberg's disease: Osteochondritis of the second and third metatarsal head epiphyses.

Gangrene: Death of tissue due to loss of blood supply.

Gastroscopy: Examination of the stomach by direct visual inspection through a special instrument passed down the oesophagus.

Gigantism: A condition caused by a pituitary tumour.

Glioma: A tumour arising from the supporting tissue of the nervous system.

Glycosuria: Sugar in the urine.

Goitre: Thyroid enlargement.

Gout: A disease characterized by inflammatory changes in the joints caused by defective uric acid metabolism.

Grand mal: A type of epilepsy (major).

Gravid: Pregnant.

Greenstick fracture: The splitting or bending of a bone (like a green twig), which occurs in young persons.

Haemangioma: A tumour of vascular tissue.

Haematemesis: Vomiting of blood.

Haematoma: A swelling caused by a localized collection of blood.

Haematuria: Blood in the urine.

Haemoptysis: The coughing-up of blood.

Hallux valgus: Deviation of the big toe towards the other toes.

Hemiplegia: Paralysis of one side of the body.

Hepatitis: Inflammation of the liver.

Hernia: The protrusion of any organ from its normal surroundings.

Hiatus hernia: Protrusion of an abdominal organ through the oesophageal opening in the diaphragm into the chest.

Hirschsprung's disease: Congenital megacolon.

Hodgkin's disease (lymphadenoma): A disease of the lymphatic organs.

Hydatid cyst: Cyst formation produced by infestation with a species of tape-worm.

Hydatidiform mole: A cyst-like tumour arising from an abnormal placenta.

Hydramnios: An excessive amount of amniotic fluid in the uterus.

Hydrocephalus: An excess of cerebrospinal fluid within the skull.

Hydronephrosis: Enlargement of the renal pelvis and calices, resulting from obstruction below.

Hydropneumothorax: The presence of fluid and air in the pleural cavity.

Hydrothorax: Fluid in the pleural cavity.

Hyperaemia: Excessive blood in a part of the body.

Hyperglycaemia: Excessive sugar in the blood.

Hypernephroma: A neoplasm of the renal parenchyma.

Hyperplasia: Tissue enlargement.

Hypertension: Raised blood pressure.

Hypertonic: Having an excessive muscular tone.

Hypertrophy: Abnormal enlargement of an organ due to increase in its tissue.

Hypoplasia: Underdevelopment.

Hypotonic: Having a decreased muscular tone.

Idiopathic (disease): Of unknown origin.

Ileitis: Inflammation of the ileum.

Ileostomy: An artificial opening of the ileum on to the anterior abdominal wall.

Ileus: Partial or complete intestinal obstruction.

Infarction: Death of tissues due to sudden blocking of a terminal artery.

Inflammation: The local reaction of the body to any form of damage to its cells.

Intussusception: A condition in which a portion of bowel prolapses into a part immediately adjoining it.

Ischaemia: A localized deficiency of blood in a part of the body.

Jaundice: A yellowing of the skin because of excessive bilirubin being present in the circulating blood.

Kienbock's disease: Osteochondritis of the carpal lunate bone.

Klippel–Feil syndrome: Congenital fusion of several cervical vertebrae, usually with associated spina bifida.

Koch's disease: Tuberculosis.

Kohler's disease: Osteochondritis of the tarsal navicular bone.

Kyphosis (humpback): An exaggeration of the normal dorsal backward curvature of the spine.

Laminectomy: Removal of one or more vertebral laminae in order to gain access to the interior of the vertebral canal.

Lesion: Damage to a body structure due to injury or disease.

Leucocyte: A white blood-cell.

Leucocytosis: An increase in the number of leucocytes.

Leucotomy: The cutting of certain nerve fibres in the frontal lobes of the brain as a form of treatment for some forms of severe mental disorders, e.g. schizophrenia.

Leukaemia: A malignant disease of the blood-forming tissues with excessive production of the white cell elements.

Lipoma: A benign tumour which develops from fat cells of subcutaneous tissue.

Lithiasis: Stone formation.

Lobectomy: Surgical removal of a lobe of a lung.

Lordosis: Exaggeration of the normal lumbar forward curvature of the spine.

Lumbago: Pain in the lumbar region of the spine.

Lymphadenoma: Hodgkin's disease (q.v.).

Lymphoma: Malignant tumour of lymphoid tissue.

Malaise: A feeling of being unwell.

Malignant: An infiltrating tumour producing secondary effects elsewhere in the body (see Metastasis).

March fracture: Fracture of a metatarsal resulting from abnormal but minor stress.

Mastectomy: Removal of a breast.

Mastoidectomy: Surgical operation on the mastoid air cells.

Meckel's diverticulum: A congenital diverticulum in the lower ileum.

Medulloblastoma: A type of intracranial neoplasm.

Megacolon: Dilatation of part or the whole of the colon.

Melaena: Black, tarry stools due to the presence of altered blood.

Melanoma: A tumour of cells which produce pigment. It may be simple (a mole), or undergo malignant change into a malignant melanoma.

Menière's disease: A disease of the inner ear causing dizziness, deafness and vomiting.

Meninges: Membranes covering the brain and spinal cord.

Meningioma: A benign tumour arising from the meninges.

Meningitis: Inflammation of the meninges.

Meningocoele: Protrusion of the meninges through a defect either in the skull or spinal column, forming a cyst.

Meniscectomy: Removal of a joint cartilage from the knee.

Menopause: Cessation of menstrual periods.

Menorrhagia: Excessive loss of blood during menstrual periods.

Metastasis: A secondary growth arising from a primary malignant tumour elsewhere.

Migraine: A type of paroxysmal headache often accompanied with vomiting.

Miliary (like millet seeds): Used to describe multiple small, discrete foci of disease, uniformly distributed.

Mitral regurgitation: Back-flow of blood through the mitral valve.

Mitral stenosis: Narrowing of the mitral valve.

Multigravida: A woman who has had one or more previous pregnancies.

Multipara: A woman who has given birth to more than one child.

Mumps: A form of acute infection of the salivary gland, usually the parotid.

Myasthenia gravis: A disease associated with severe muscle weakness.

Myeloma, multiple: A disease characterized by multiple malignant tumours arising from bone marrow cells.

Myocarditis: Inflammation of the myocardium.

Myocardium: Heart muscle.

Myositis ossificans: Calcification in a haematoma in a muscle.

Myxoedema: A disease due to under-activity of the thyroid gland.

Naevus: A birthmark, a mole.

Necrosis: Cellular death involving circumscribed areas of tissue.

Neoplasm: New growth (tumour).

Nephrectomy: Removal of a kidney.

Nephritis: Inflammation of the kidneys.

Nephrocalcinosis: A condition in which numerous small deposits of calcium are found in the medulla of the kidneys.

Nephrostomy: Surgical drainage of the renal pelvis.

Neuralgia: Pain along the course of a nerve.

Neuroblastoma: A highly malignant tumour in children arising from the adrenal medulla.

Neurofibroma: A benign tumour arising from the fibrous sheath of a nerve.

Neurofibromatosis: The development of multiple neurofibromas.

Nodule: A small swelling.

Oedema: An excess of fluid in the tissues.

Oesophageal varices: Dilated veins at the lower end of the oesophagus.

Oesophagoscopy: Examination of the oesophagus by direct visual inspection through a special instrument.

Osgood–Schlatter's disease: Osteochondritis of the tibial tubercle epiphysis.

Osteitis: Inflammation in any part of a bone.

Osteoarthritis: A chronic degenerative type of arthritis.

Osteochondritis: A condition in which localized death of bone or cartilage cells occurs in primary or secondary ossification centres, probably as a result of a defective blood supply.

Osteochondroma: A benign tumour composed of bone and cartilage.

Osteoclastoma: A type of tumour of bone.

Osteogenesis imperfecta: Defective bone formation of the whole skeleton causing fragile, easily fractured bones.

Osteoma: A benign tumour of bone.

Osteomalacia: Softening of the bone (caused by lack of calcium and phosphorus), often associated with vitamin-D deficiency in adults.

Osteomyelitis: Inflammation of the bone.

Osteoporosis: Thinning of bony tissue caused by osteoclastic activity being greater than osteoblastic.

Otalgia: Pain in the ear.

Otitis media: Inflammation of the middle ear.

Otorrhoea: Discharge from the ear.

Paget's disease (osteitis deformans): A chronic disease of bone causing enlargement and deformity.

Pancreatitis: Inflammation of the pancreas.

Papilloedema: Swelling of the optic disk due to raised intracranial pressure.

Papilloma: A localized overgrowth of epithelium with a connective tissue core.

Paracentesis: Aspiration of fluid from a body cavity, e.g., pleura.

Paraplegia: Paralysis of both lower limbs.

Parkinson's disease (paralysis agitans): A degenerative brain disease characterized by tremor and rigidity of the head and limbs.

Pellegrini–Steida disease: The formation of a small plaque of bone in the soft tissues close to the medial condyle of the femur, following injury.

Peptic ulcer: An ulcer in the stomach or duodenum.

Perforation: Usually a perforation of the stomach or duodenal wall by an ulcerative process, or of a colonic diverticulum.

Pericardial effusion: An effusion between the two layers of the pericardium.

Pericarditis: Inflammation of the pericardium of the heart.

Peritonitis: Inflammation of the peritoneum.

Perthes' disease: Osteochondritis of the femoral head epiphysis.

Petit mal: A type of epilepsy (minor).

Phaeochromocytoma: A neoplasm of the adrenal medulla.

Phlebitis: Inflammation of a vein.

Phlebolith: Calcified thrombus within a vein.

Phthisis: Tuberculosis.

Placenta praevia: A placenta with an abnormal site of attachment in the lower segment of the uterus.

Pleural effusion: Fluid in the pleural cavity.

Pleurisy: Inflammation of the pleura.

Pneumoconiosis: Disease of the lungs caused by inhalation of industrial dust.

Pneumonectomy: Removal of a lung.

Pneumonia: Inflammation of the lung(s).

Pneumoperitoneum: The presence of air or other gas in the peritoneal cavity.

Pneumothorax: The presence of air or other gas in the pleural cavity.

Poliomyelitis: Inflammation of the grey matter in the spinal cord.

Polycythaemia: Excess red blood-cells in the circulation.

Polydactyly: Congenital presence of extra digits.

Polyp: A tumour which has a stalk.

Polyuria: The passage of excessive amounts of urine.

Pott's fracture: Fracture of the lower end of the tibia and fibula.

Pott's disease: Tuberculosis of the spine.

Precordium: The area of the chest overlying the heart.

Primary neoplasm: A tumour at its site of origin.

Primigravida: A woman who is pregnant for the first time.

Primipara: A woman who has borne her first child.

Prolapse: The abnormal descent of a structure, e.g., uterus.

Prostatectomy: Removal of the prostate gland.

Psoriasis: A skin disease characterized by scaly red patches.

Puerperium: The period immediately following labour.

Pyelitis: Inflammation of the pelvis of the kidney.

Pyelonephritis: Inflammation of the pelvis and calices of the kidney.

Pyloric stenosis: Narrowing of the pyloric canal.

Pylorospasm: Spasm of the pyloric canal.

Pyogenic: Pus producing.

Pyrexia: Raised temperature (fever).

Quadriplegia: Paralysis of all four limbs.

Regional enteritis: Crohn's disease (q.v.).

Reticulosis: A disease of the reticulo-endothelial system.

Rheumatic fever: A disease affecting connective tissue, particularly the heart and its valves, and joints.

Rheumatoid arthritis: A chronic inflammatory type of arthritis affecting a number of joints.

Rhinorrhoea: A discharge from the nose.

Rickets: A childhood disease due to lack of vitamin D, characterized by softening and deformity of bones.

Rugae: Wrinkles or corrugations, e.g., in the stomach lining.

St Vitus's dance: Chorea (q.v.).

Salpingitis: Inflammation of the Fallopian tubes.

Sarcoidosis: A chronic inflammatory disease of unknown origin.

Sarcoma: A malignant growth arising from the connective tissue of the body.

Scheuermann's disease: Osteochondritis of the vertebral epiphyseal plates.

Sciatica: Pain along the course of the sciatic nerve.

Sclerosis, disseminated, multiple: A disease characterized by widespread lesions in the brain and spinal cord.

Scoliosis: Lateral curvature of the spine.

Secondary: *See* Metastasis.

Seminoma: A neoplasm of the testis.

Shingles (Herpes Zoster): A viral disease of the nervous system closely related to chicken-pox.

Sigmoidoscopy: Examination of the interior of the lower bowel by direct vision through a special instrument.

Sign: An abnormality detected during the course of a medical examination.

Silicosis: *See* Pneumoconiosis.

Sinus: 1. A track leading from an abscess.
     2. A venous channel in the skull.
     3. A cavity within a bone.

Sinusitis: Inflammation of the nasal accessory sinuses.

Smith's fracture: Fracture of the lower end of the radius with anterior displacement of the lower fragment.

Spalding's sign: Over-riding of the fetal skull bones *in utero*. Associated with fetal death.

Spasm: A violent muscular contraction.

Spina bifida: The failure of the posterior neural arch of a vertebra to develop and unite.

Splenomegaly: Enlargement of the spleen.

Spondylitis, ankylosing: *See* Ankylosing spondylitis.

Spondylolisthesis: Slipping forward of a vertebra on the body of the one below it.

Spondylosis: Arthritis of the spine.

Status asthmaticus: An asthmatic attack lasting over a period of several days.

Stenosis: Narrowing.

Still's disease: A type of childhood rheumatoid arthritis.

Stress fracture: Fracture due to abnormal minor stress on a bone.

Stress incontinence: Involuntary passing of urine when the abdominal pressure is raised (e.g., by coughing).

Stricture: Narrowing of a passage.

Stroke: An acute condition causing fainting and paralysis as a result of a cerebrovascular lesion (haemorrhage, embolism or thrombosis).

Subluxation: Incomplete dislocation.

Supracondylar fracture: Fracture just above the condyles of the femur or humerus.

Surgical emphysema: The presence of air in the subcutaneous tissues.

Symptom: An abnormality detected by the patient himself.

Syndrome: A combination of symptoms and signs forming a recognizable disease pattern.

Tachycardia: Abnormal rapidity of the heart-beat.

Tenosynovitis: Inflammation of a tendon-sheath.

Teratoma: A complex tumour containing a variety of tissue such as hair, teeth, brain, muscle, etc.

Tetraplegia: Paralysis of all four limbs.

Thoracoplasty: An operation which involves removing a number of ribs together with part of the underlying lung.

Thoracotomy: A surgical opening into the thoracic cavity.

Thrombocytopaenia: A deficiency of platelets in circulation.

Thrombophlebitis: A disease in which inflammatory changes in walls of veins result in thrombus formation.

Thrombosis: Formation of a clot within a blood-vessel.

Thrombus: A clot.

Thyrotoxicosis: A disease due to over-activity of the thyroid gland.

Tinnitus: Buzzing or ringing noises in the head.

Torticollis: Spasm of the neck muscles, resulting in twisting of the neck.

Trauma: Injury.

Tubercles: Inflammatory tuberculous nodules.

Tuberculosis: Infection with acid-fast (*Mycobacterium tuberculosis*) bacilli.

Tumour: Neoplasm or new growth.

Ulcer: An open sore of skin or mucous membrane.

Uraemia: Symptoms due to the accumulation of toxic substances in the blood-stream, due to failure of excretion.

Vagotomy: Cutting of the vagus nerves to reduce the secretion of acid by the stomach, and also the motility of the stomach.

Varices: Dilated veins.

Varicose veins: Dilated veins which pursue a tortuous path.

Vertigo: Dizziness.

Vesical calculus: A bladder stone.

Volvulus: Twisting of the bowel on itself, producing obstruction.

Wassermann test: A test to indicate the presence of syphilis.

Wilms's tumour: A malignant kidney tumour of young children.

Xanthomatosis: A lipid storage disease causing multiple areas of bony destruction.

PREFIXES

A-: Absence or deficiency.

An-: Absence or deficiency.

Angio-: Pertaining to blood-vessels.

Arterio-: Pertaining to arteries.

Arthr-: Pertaining to joints.

Bronch-: Pertaining to the bronchi.

Cardi-: Pertaining to the heart.

Chol-: Pertaining to the bile.

Chondro-: Pertaining to cartilage.

Crani-: Pertaining to the cranium.

Cyst-: A bladder.

Derm-: Pertaining to the skin.

Dys-: Difficulty.

Ec-: Outside the normal position.
Enceph-: Pertaining to the brain.
Endo-: Inside.
Epi-: On top of.
Ex-: Out.
Gastr-: Pertaining to the stomach.
Haem-: Pertaining to blood.
Hepa-: Pertaining to the liver.
Hydro-: Fluid.
Hyper-: Increased.
Hypo-: Decreased.
Infra-: Below.
Leuco-: Pertaining to the white blood-corpuscles.
Lymph-: Pertaining to the lymphatic system.
Myo-: Pertaining to muscle.
Neo-: New.
Nephr-: Pertaining to the kidney.
Neuro-: Pertaining to the nervous system.
Oeso-: Pertaining to the oesophagus.
Osteo-: Pertaining to bones.
Peri-: Adjacent to.
Phleb-: Pertaining to veins.
Pneumo-: Pertaining to the lungs.
Poly-: Multiple.
Post-: After.
Pre-: Before.
Py-: Pus.
Sial-: Pertaining to the salivary glands.
Spondyl-: Pertaining to a vertebra.
Sub-: Below.
Supra-: Above.
Thora-: Pertaining to the thorax.
Thromb-: Pertaining to clotting of blood.
Trach-: Pertaining to the trachea.
Vesico-: Pertaining to the bladder.

SUFFIXES

-ectomy: Surgical removal.
-itis: Inflammation.
-lithiasis: Stone formation.
-oscopy: Visual examination.
-ostomy: Making an opening into.
-otomy: Incising into or through.

Appendix 3

COMMON ABBREVIATIONS

AE	After evacuation
AEG	Air encephalogram
AFB	Acid-fast (tubercle) bacilli
AFM	After fatty meal
AM	After micturition
AP	Anteroposterior *or*
	Artificial pneumothorax
ASD	Atrial septal defect
AV	Arteriovenous (anomaly)
BI	Bone injury
BP	Blood-pressure
BS	Breath sounds
BSR	Blood sedimentation rate
Ca	Carcinoma
CAT	Computerized axial tomography
CBD	Common bile-duct
CCF	Congestive cardiac failure
CDH	Congenital dislocation of hip
CNS	Central nervous system
CO	Complaining of
COAD	Chronic obstructive airways disease
CSF	Cerebrospinal fluid
CSOM	Chronic suppurative otitis media
CSU	Catheter specimen of urine
CT	Coronary thrombosis *or*
	Cerebral thrombosis *or*
	Computerized tomography
CVA	Cerebrovascular accident
D & C	Dilatation and curettage
DM	Diabetes mellitus
DU	Duodenal ulcer
DSA	Digital subtraction angiography
DVI	Digital vascular imaging
DVT	Deep venous thrombosis
ECG	Electrocardiogram
ECT	Electroconvulsive therapy

EDC	Expected date of confinement
EDD	Expected date of delivery
EEG	Electro-encephalogram
EP	Epilepsy *or*
	Eclampsia of pregnancy
ERCP	Endoscopic retrograde cholangiography and pancreatography
ESR	Erythrocyte sedimentation rate
EUA	Examination under anaesthetic
#	Fracture
FB	Foreign body
FH	Family history
FO	Fronto-occipital
GIT	Gastrointestinal tract
GU	Gastric ulcer *or*
	Genito-urinary
HPC	History of present condition
IAM	Internal auditory meatus
IDK	Internal derangement of the knee
IOFB	Intra-ocular foreign body
ISQ	As before (*in status quo*)
IUCD	Intra-uterine contraceptive device
IUD	Intra-uterine death
IV	Intravenous *or*
	Intervertebral
KUB	Kidneys, ureters and bladder
LA	Left auricle or atrium
LAO	Left anterior oblique
LB	Loose body
LIF	Left iliac fossa
LLL	Left lower lobe
LLZ	Left lower zone
LMP	Last menstrual period
LMZ	Left middle zone
LOA	Left occipito-anterior
LOP	Left occipitoposterior
LOT	Left occipitotransverse
LP	Lumbar puncture
LSA	Left sacro-anterior

LSP	Left sacroposterior
LUL	Left upper lobe
LUZ	Left upper zone
LV	Left ventricle
LVF	Left ventricular failure
MC	Metacarpal
MCP	Metacarpophalangeal
MI	Myocardial infarct
MRI	Magnetic resonance imaging
MS	Mitral stenosis
MT	Metatarsal
MTP	Metatarsophalangeal
MVD	Mitral valve disease
NAD	Nil abnormal detected
NFS	No fracture shown
NG	New growth (neoplasm)
NMR	Nuclear magnetic resonance
NPN	Non-protein nitrogen
NPU	Not passed urine
NYD	Not yet diagnosed
OA	Osteoarthritis
OE	On examination
OF	Occipitofrontal
OM	Occipitomental
PA	Postero-anterior *or* Pernicious anaemia
PET	Positron emission tomography
PGE	Posterior gastro-enterostomy
Ph ($\phi\theta$)	Phthisis (tuberculosis)
PH	Personal history
PI	Past illness
PID	Prolapsed intervertebral disk
PM	Postmicturition
PN	Percussion note
PNS	Postnasal space
POP	Plaster-of-Paris *or* Persistent occipitoposterior
PP	Pneumoperitoneum *or* Proximal phalanx
PR	Per rectum *or* Post reduction

PTA	Percutaneous transluminal angioplasty
PTB	Pulmonary tuberculosis
PTC	Percutaneous transhepatic cholangiography
PU	Peptic ulcer *or*
	Passed urine
PUO	Pyrexia of unknown origin
PV	Per vaginam
qv	please see (*quod vide*)
RA	Right auricle or atrium *or*
	Rheumatoid arthritis
RAO	Right anterior oblique
RHD	Rheumatic heart disease
RIF	Right iliac fossa
RLL	Right lower lobe
RLZ	Right lower zone
RML	Right middle lobe
RMZ	Right middle zone
ROA	Right occipito-anterior
ROP	Right occipitoposterior
ROT	Right occipitotransverse
RSA	Right sacroanterior
RSP	Right sacroposterior
RST	Right sacrotransverse
RTA	Road traffic accident
RUL	Right upper lobe
RUZ	Right upper zone
RV	Right ventricle
SAH	Subarachnoid haemorrhage
SI	Sacro-iliac
SMV	Submentovertical
SOL	Space-occupying lesion
SOM	Suppurative otitis media *or*
	Suboccipitomental
SPECT	Single photon emission computerized tomography
TB	Tuberculosis
TIA	Transient ischaemic attack
TMJ	Temporomandibular joint
TP	Terminal phalanx
TPR	Temperature, pulse, and respiration
URTI	Upper respiratory tract infection

| VSD | Ventricular septal defect |
| WR | Wassermann reaction |

Appendix 4

RADIO-ISOTOPE IMAGING

These examinations depend on the use of radioactive substances which are designed to be taken up by particular organs when introduced into the body, usually intravenously. There are many suitable radiopharmaceuticals available, but this section will be limited to those based on technetium 99 ($^{99}Tc^m$), which has a half-life of 6 hr and which decays with the emission of gamma rays only with an energy of 140 keV. The emitted radiation can be detected by various means, but for imaging purposes the principal apparatus now in use is the gamma camera. The technetium is obtained by eluting a 'generator' which contains ^{99}Mo adsorbed on to an alumina column. The eluate is in the form of sodium pertechnetate. It may be used in this form, or after being incorporated into other preparations, usually by means of 'kits' supplied by nuclear medicine specialist firms.

Positioning nomenclature is different from that used in radiography since the radiation originates from within the patient, and the position is named by that region of the body which is nearest the detector. All gamma cameras have a persistence scope so that gross positioning can be checked before imaging commences. Generally speaking, positioning is not necessarily as acute as in radiography, but should be standardized in order to allow results to be reproduced.

Exposures may be determined either by the amount of radiation (counts) reaching the detector, or by the length of time counting takes place, or by a combination of the two, the exposure terminating when the first of the two pre-set criteria are reached.

The following list of examinations will serve as a guide line to those examinations which will probably constitute the vast majority of the work in a nuclear medical imaging department in a district general hospital.

ABDOMEN. Radiopharmaceutical: Pertechnetate ($^{99}Tc^mO_4$).
  Dose. 200 MBq (5 mCi approx). Radiation dose 25 mGy (2·5 rad) to thyroid, 0·25 mGy (0·025 rad) whole body.

  The pertechnetate is trapped by gastric mucosa, and the stomach can be imaged if required. However, it is usual to carry out this investigation to determine the presence or absence of a Meckel's diverticulum which contains ectopic gastric mucosa and hence may be visualized.

Technique. The whole abdomen is imaged in the anterior position with the patient supine. Films should be taken at 1-minute intervals up to 15 min, and then at 20, 25 and 30 min. Finally a lateral film of the abdomen is taken immediately after the 30 min film. Suggested exposure 1 min per image.

Preparation. It may be thought desirable to give the patient 200 mg cimetidine three times on the day before the examination, and 400 mg on the morning of the examination.

BONE. Radiopharmaceutical: $^{99}Tc^m$ MDP (methylene diphosphonate).

Dose. 400 MBq (10 mCi approx.). Radiation dose: 5 mGy (0·5 rad) to bone, 10 mGy (1 rad) to kidneys.

Technique. Imaging is carried out 2–4 hours after injection. The radio-isotope that is not incorporated into bone by osteoblastic activity is removed from the blood pool by the kidneys, hence delayed films may show enhanced contrast because the background radiation from the tissues is less. Against this, however, must be considered the relatively short half-life of the isotope and its consequent diminishing activity with time.

Because of the way the isotope is incorporated into the bones, sites that are undergoing increased osteoblastic activity, whether as a result of malignant disease or healing fractures, etc., will show as areas of increased uptake on the films.

It is usual to image the entire skeleton with the exception of the upper and lower limbs unless there is any specific reason for these to be included. Since the isotope is excreted by the kidneys the patient's bladder should be emptied prior to taking the views of the pelvis.

Suggested exposure: 200 000–300 000 counts per view.

Positioning. The number of views required to cover the skeleton will depend on the size of the gamma camera. A normal large-field camera will require 7 or 8 exposures, a suitable series being:

Both lateral skulls, which will include oblique views of the cervical vertebrae.

Both posterior shoulders, to include the ribs and thoracic vertebrae.

Anterior of sternum and ribs.

Posterior of the lower thoracic and lumbar vertebrae.

Anterior and posterior views of the pelvis and hips.

BRAIN. Radiopharmaceutical: $^{99}Tc^m$ DTPA (diethyl-triamino-penta-acetic acid).

Dose. 400 MBq (10 mCi approx.). Radiation dose 1 mGy (0·1 rad) to whole body, 30 mGy (3·0 rad) to kidneys.

A suitable alternative to DTPA is glucoheptonate. Some centres use the sodium pertechnetate straight from the generator, but in these cases the patient must have a premedication of sodium or potassium perchlorate (400 mg orally, 30 min before imaging), in order to block uptake of the pertechnetate by the thyroid, salivary glands and choroid plexuses.

The detection of tumours and vascular abnormalities in the brain relies on the local disturbance of the microcirculation at the site of the lesion. Dynamic studies may be performed to demonstrate relative circulation between the two hemispheres, and static studies are routinely made in five projections approximately 30 min after injection, although delayed films at 2–3 hr may demonstrate lesions not adequately visualized earlier.

Technique

Dynamic studies: Although a computer is often used for these series, it is not absolutely essential, and a good visual impression is often gained from a direct micro-dot series. The exposures should last over a period of about 30 sec commencing from the injection, which should be as rapid as possible and preferably 'chased' by about 10–20 ml saline. A suggested series would be of 16–24 films of 1½–2 sec each. Alternatively a video tape-recorder can be used to record the series for subsequent replay and analysis.

The patient may be in either the posterior or vertex position (for positioning *see* Static studies, *below*). The posterior is useful for detecting subdural haematomas and other vascular lesions, and the vertex position for comparing cerebral perfusion.

Static studies: Five projections are routinely taken. Exposure may be determined either by count or time. In the absence of a converging collimator which will enable only the skull with the minimum of facial area to be included on the film, it is probably better to expose for a predetermined time, since the inclusion of a large area of the face which is very vascular, will appreciably affect the count rate.

Suggested exposure time: 3–5 min per view, although in the case of uncooperative patients it may be necessary to reduce this. Probably about 1½ min is the least time in which a satisfactory image can be built up.

Positioning
1. Lateral. Patient seated or prone, the head resting against the detector, with the sagittal plane parallel to it. Both laterals are taken.
2. Anterior. Patient seated or prone, the nose and forehead rest on the detector, with the sagittal plane perpendicular to it.
3. Posterior. Patient seated or supine, the occiput rests on the detector with the sagittal plane perpendicular to it. The radiographic base line should also be perpendicular to the detector even if this means slightly raising the head on a foam pad, since this will help visualization of the posterior fossa.
4. Vertex. Patient supine with the vertex resting against the detector, the sagittal plane perpendicular and the radiographic base line parallel to it. A lead-rubber cape is placed around the neck and over the shoulders to minimize radiation from the rest of the body reaching the detector.

Note: Owing to the versatility of the gamma camera and the fact that the radiation originates inside the patient, all positioning is capable of appreciable modification when required, and all views may be made with the patient supine.

GALLBLADDER AND BILIARY TRACT. Radiopharmaceutical: $^{99}Tc^m$-labelled HIDA (Hepatic Iminodiacetic acid). A number of compounds are available with broadly similar properties.

Dose. 80 MBq. Radiation dose 8 mGy (0·8 rad) to gallbladder, 0·4 mGy (0·04 rad) whole body, approx.

Preparation. The patient is fasted for at least 4 hr prior to the examination.

Technique. Images are taken at 10–15 min intervals for 1 hr. During this time the gallbladder should fill, and the radionuclide may or may not be seen in the small bowel. If it is desired to check the gallbladder emptying rate after the stimulus of a fatty-meal, half a pint of milk can be given at this stage, and images taken at 5-min intervals for the next hour. Regions of interest may be drawn round the gallbladder to calculate activity, and this plotted against time to give a graphical indication of emptying rate. Suggested exposure 1 min per image.

G.I.T. BLEED. Two techniques are available. If it is known that there is appreciable bleeding it is quicker to inject a colloid, as for liver imaging. This is cleared rapidly from the blood pool, with a half clearance time of 2½ min. Exposures should be made at 2-min intervals for 30 min. Suggested exposure 1 min per image. If during that time some radionuclide is transferred into the gastrointestinal tract through a bleeding point, it will quickly become visible against an increasingly 'cold' abdomen. If bleeding is suspected to be slight, this technique may not be positive, and as an alternative the following may be tried.

The patient is given an injection of a proprietary stannous agent for red-blood cell labelling, followed 20 min later by 800 MBq of pertechnetate. This is automatically tagged on to the red blood cells *in vivo*, and in theory, the activity now stays within the blood pool. Imaging can take place over an extended period, and any bleeding that occurs during that period, will show as a 'pooling' within the gastrointestinal tract. Imaging can be continued for up to 24 hr. Images should be of 1 million counts, which will be less than a minute initially, but take about 15 min at 24 hr.

LIVER AND SPLEEN. Radiopharmaceutical: $^{99}Tc^m$-labelled sulphur colloid.

Dose. 80 MBq (2 mCi approx.). Radiation dose 6 mGy (0·6 rad) to liver, 1 mGy (0·1 rad) whole body.

The particle size of the colloid is such that it is taken up by the reticulo-endothelial system in the liver and spleen. If there is an appreciable degree of cirrhosis of the liver the surplus colloid may be taken up by the reticulo-endothelial system in the bone marrow also.

Technique. Static studies are taken in four positions commencing approximately 10 min after the injection. Suggested exposure: 300 000 counts per view.

Positioning. Anterior, posterior and both laterals are taken, inclusion of the entire liver and spleen being checked with reference to the persistence scope, it is helpful to mark the level of the lower costal margin on the anterior view, using an appropriate radioactive marker.

LUNG. Ventilation and perfusion studies are possible. Ideally ventilation studies should be performed whenever there is a defect on the perfusion scan. However, this is subject to the availability of a rubidium/krypton generator, or radioaerosol system.

Perfusion studies. Radiopharmaceutical: $^{99}Tc^m$-labelled micro-spheres or microaggregates.

Dose. 80 MBq (2 mCi approx.). Radiation dose 8 mGy (0·8 rad) to lungs and liver.

Note. This is one of the few examinations for which there are known hazards. Pulmonary oedema is a contraindication, as is a known sensitivity to albumens.

The particle sizes of these radiopharmaceuticals are such that they are too large to pass through the capillaries of the lungs, hence by capillary blockade they give an indication of the blood supply to the lungs.

Technique. Four views are routinely taken, commencing about 5 min after the injection. Suggested exposure: 300 000 counts per view.

Positioning. Anterior, posterior and both laterals are taken, the inclusion of the entire lung fields being checked with reference to the persistence scope. In addition, posterior oblique views with the patient rotated 45–50° may provide useful supplementary information.

RENAL. Two types of studies are possible. Static imaging to show renal size and shape, and dynamic imaging (renography) to indicate renal function.

Static studies. Radiopharmaceutical: $^{99}Tc^m$ DMSA (dimer-captosuccinic acid).

Dose. 80 MBq (2 mCi approx.). Radiation dose 28 mGy (2·8 rad) to kidney.

This preparation is taken up very efficiently by the renal tubular cells but only slowly excreted, hence it gives a good indication of the functioning tubular mass and relative uptake in each kidney reflects its function.

Technique. Only one exposure is usually taken, 2–3 hr after the injection. Suggested exposure 300 000 counts.

Positioning. Posterior.

Dynamic studies. Radiopharmaceutical: $^{99}Tc^m$ DTPA (diethyl-triamino-penta-acetic acid).

Dose. 160 MBq (4 mCi approx.). Radiation dose 12 mGy (1·2 rad) to kidney.

This preparation is excreted by glomerular filtration and is an alternative to ^{131}I or ^{123}I hippuran. Where pelviureteric junction obstruction is suspected, a diuretic may be given towards the end of the series, thus differentiating between genuine obstruction and hypotonia. Frusemide 0·5 mg kg is the diuretic generally used.

Technique. The use of a computer-controlled data-logger is essential. The series should continue for approximately 30 min or in the case of a diuresis renogram, 40 min with the

Frusemide injected at about 20 min. The patient is seated with his back to the detector which is positioned so that the entire renal tract will be included in the field of view. (In order to maintain the patient's stability for such a period it may be arranged to sit the patient on a chair with side arms from which the back-rest has been removed.)

Exact exposure suggestions are impossible and will vary with the data acquisition unit available, but a typical series would consist of 20-sec frames for the duration of the examination, commencing with the injection.

Following the examination, regions of interest may be drawn around each kidney and the bladder and, following background subtraction, curves drawn to indicate the relative excretions of the two kidneys and their response, if any, to the diuretic.

THYROID.   Radiopharmaceutical: pertechnetate ($^{99}Tc^mO_4$).

Dose.   80 MBq (2 mCi approx.). Radiation dose 10 mGy (1 rad) to thyroid, 0.1 mGy (0.01 rad) whole body.

This preparation is taken up by the thyroid iodide trap but it is not incorporated into hormones and retained. The examination will usually differentiate between hot and cold nodules, the latter requiring ultrasound examination to differentiate further between solid and cystic lesions.

Technique.   Ideally a pinhole collimator should be used (3 mm diameter), at a standard distance above the patient, so that enlargement is constant for all patients, and if necessary thyroid size can be estimated.

Exposure should be by time rather than count, as this will give an indication of the function of the thyroid. Only one exposure is necessary. Suggested exposure: 6–10 min.

Positioning.   Anterior. The patient is placed supine with the chin slightly raised, and the collimator positioned in the mid-line about 5 cm (2 in) above the sternal notch.

Appendix 5

NAMED VIEWS OF THE SKULL

It is impossible to include all the named views in this list and the following is only intended as a guide to help radiographers should a specific view be requested. The use of names for the routine views is not to be recommended, but may be justifiable in the lesser-used ones. Angles of tilt and rotation vary slightly from one description to another and those given here are the most frequently used.

Some originators also gave their name to more than one view (i.e., Law, Schüller), and the description given here is the more commonly accepted.

ALBERS-SCHÖNBERG. To demonstrate the temporomandibular joints.

Head in the true lateral position, then rotated 20° towards the face. Centre to the temporomandibular joint in contact with the film, with the tube angled 20° towards the head.

ARCELIN. To demonstrate the petrous temporal region.

Head AP, rotated 45° away from the side being examined, with the radiographic base-line at right-angles to the film. Centre to the radiographic base-line at a point 1 in (2·5 cm) in front of the external auditory meatus, with the tube angled 10° to the feet.

BERTEL. To demonstrate the orbital floors and the infraorbital fissure.

Head in the true PA position with the radiographic base-line at right-angles to the film. Centre to the nasion with the tube angled 20° towards the head.

CAHOON. To demonstrate the styloid processes.

Position as in Bertel (*above*) but with the tube angled 25° towards the head.

CALDWELL. This is the routine 20° occipitofrontal view (*see* SKULL).

DUTT (Johnson and Dutt). This is the PA oblique view for cribriform plate (q.v.).

HAAS.   To demonstrate the petrous temporal region, foramen magnum, and dorsum sellae.

Head in the true PA position with the radiographic base-line at right-angles to the film. Centre in the midline to the external occipital protuberance with the tube angled 45° towards the head.

HENSCHEN.   To demonstrate the petrous temporal region.

Head in the true lateral position. Centre 2 in (5 cm) above the external auditory meatus away from the film, with the tube angled 15° towards the feet.

HICKEY.   This is the profile view of the mastoid region (*see* MASTOIDS).

HIRTZ.   This is the routine submentovertical (axial) position (*see* SKULL).

JOHNSON AND DUTT.   This is the PA oblique view for cribriform plate (q.v.).

LAW.   To demonstrate the petrous temporal region.

Head in the true lateral position, then rotated 15° towards the face. Centre 2 in (5 cm) above and 2 in behind the external auditory meatus away from the film with the tube tilted 15° towards the feet.

MAY.   To demonstrate the zygomatic arch.

Head in the PA position with the chin tilted as far up as possible, and resting on the film. The head is then rotated 15° away from the side being examined. Centre through the zygomatic arch, with the tube angled towards the feet so that the central ray is at right-angles to the radiographic base-line.

MAYER.   To demonstrate the petrous temporal region.

Patient in the AP position with the radiographic base-line at right-angles to the film. Rotate the head 45° towards the side being examined, and centre through the external auditory meatus nearest the film, with the tube angled 45° towards the feet.

PIRIE.   This is the routine occipitomental view with open mouth (*see* SINUSES).

RHESE.   This is the routine PA oblique view for optic foramen (q.v.).

SCHÜLLER. This is the lateral view for the petrous temporal region (q.v.).

STENVER. This is the oblique view for the petrous temporal region (q.v.).

STOCKHOLM C. This position corresponds closely to Stenver's view, but is designed for use with a skull unit, using double tube angulation, rather than patient angulation.

Head in the true lateral position, with the centre point of the bucky 1 in (2·5 cm) in front of the external auditory meatus and ½ in (1 cm) above the orbitomeatal line. The tube is angled 10° towards the head, and 30° towards the face. The grid must be rotated accordingly.

TITTERINGTON. This is the 30° occipitomental view for facial bones and the zygomatic arches (*see* FACIAL BONES).

TOWNES. This is the routine 35° fronto-occipital (half-axial) view (*see* SKULL).

VALDINI. To demonstrate the squamous portion of the occipital bone and the foramen magnum.

Heas in the PA position with the chin tucked in as far as possible and the frontal region resting on the film, with the radiographic base-line tilted 45–50° towards the feet. Centre in the midline at the level of the external auditory meatus.

WATERS. This is the routine occipitomental view for sinuses (q.v.).

Appendix 6

SOME NORMAL BLOOD VALUES

BLOOD UREA. Normal value 2·5–7·5 mmol/l (15–40 mg%).
Normal dose urography unlikely to be effective if blood urea is much above 10 mmol/l (60 mg%). High dose urography may be of value above this level, especially if the blood urea is falling rather than rising.

SERUM BILIRUBIN. Normal value 5–17 μmol/l (0·1–0·5 mg%).
Oral cholecystography unlikely to be effective above 20 μmol/l. Intravenous cholecystangiography may be effective up to 60 μmol/l. The gallbladder is more likely to show function if the level is falling rather than rising.

E.S.R. (Erythrocyte Sedimentation Rate). M 0–9 mm/hour, F 0–15 mm/hour.
If raised, it is usually an indication of disease being present.

HAEMOGLOBIN. Adult male 14–18 g/dl. Adult female 12–16 g/dl.

RED BLOOD CELLS (R.B.C.). Adult male 4·6–6·2 million/μl. Adult female 4·2–5·4 million/μl.

WHITE BLOOD CELLS (W.B.C.). 4000–10 000/μl.

Neutrophils	40–75%
Eosinophils	1–6%
Basophils	<1%
Lymphocytes	20–45%
Monocytes	2–10%

BLEEDING TIME. 2·5–7 min.

CLOTTING TIME.
(capillary) 5–7 min.
(venous) 4–7 min.

PROTHROMBIN TIME. 10–14 sec.

BLOOD SUGAR. (fasting). 3·3–6·7 mmol/l (60–100 mg/100 ml).

GUIDELINES ON THE EXPOSURE TO IONIZING RADIATION OF WOMEN WHO ARE, OR WHO MAY BE, PREGNANT

In the light of recent research findings, it has been agreed that continued application of the 10-Day Rule is not necessarily appropriate. Radiographic examinations of female patients of childbearing age, where the uterus falls within or near the useful beam, should not be confined to the first ten days of the menstrual cycle, but can proceed at any time provided that the patient is not pregnant.

Although the ultimate responsibility for the patient lies with the referring clinician and/or the radiologist, it is the responsibility of the examining radiographer to establish as far as possible that the patient is not pregnant, and to take guidance from the referring clinician and/or the radiologist if there is any doubt as to possible pregnancy.

The College of Radiographers and The Royal College of Radiologists, after consultation with The British Institute of Radiology and The National Radiological Protection Board, have agreed outline procedures which should be adapted to suit local circumstances, and they commend to each department the establishment of a departmental protocol.

Imaging Department Procedures for Diagnostic Examinations of Women of Reproductive Capacity

1. There should be an agreed procedure for each department, based on these guidelines, and displayed appropriately within the department.
2. The ultimate responsibility for the patient lies with the referring clinician and/or the radiologist.
3. It is the responsibility of the examining radiographer to ask the Pregnancy Question of any woman of reproductive capacity where the uterus may lie in or near the useful beam.
4. The examining radiographer should ensure that the Pregnancy Question is asked in private.
5. If the answer to the Pregnancy Question is other than no, the examining radiographer must contact the referring clinician and/or the radiologist for an opinion before proceeding with the examination. If it is decided that the examination is to proceed, despite the possibility or fact of

pregnancy, then the authorization for this decision must be recorded in the patient's case notes.

6. It is the responsibility of the employing authority that there is a mechanism for incorporating details of the examination into the notes of pregnant, or possibly pregnant, patients, and to make provision to store such records for the appropriate length of time.

In formulating these guidelines, the COR, RCR, BIR and NRPB are concerned to ensure that in the examination of any patient, the use of ionizing radiation is kept to a minimum at all times, and that the greatest care should always be taken to minimize the number of views and absorbed dose consistent with diagnostic needs.

Radiopharmaceuticals

This document is NOT applicable to the use of radiopharmaceuticals. An appendix will be published to cover their use as soon as possible.

See Decision Chart on next page.

Decision Chart for Use in Developing Local Guidelines for Examination of Patients who are, or who may be, Pregnant

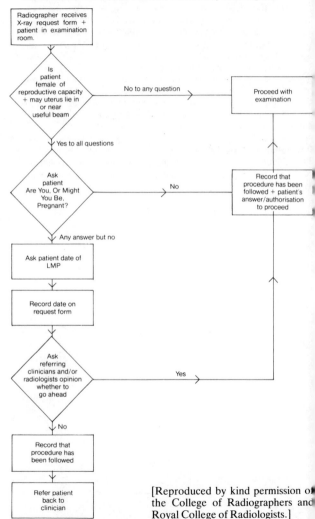

[Reproduced by kind permission of the College of Radiographers and Royal College of Radiologists.]